Praise for *The Pow‹*

"In *The Power of Humility*, the au
subject of relationships and conflic
our Highest Principle. Following a meticulous method ...
senting relevant personal stories and revealing references from diverse
sources, they have given us an outstanding argument for using humility as a way of life.

"On a personal level, what they present is immediately relevant, and
there cannot be anyone who would not benefit from reading it. On a
global level, perhaps it should be considered as essential reading for
anyone considering taking up public office—particularly politics and
religion, where the attitude of 'them versus us' is usually the default
setting.

"I hope that this book becomes a bestseller, as it offers not only a
message of hope, but one of certainty—that conflict can be resolved by
a change of perception and attitude. World peace is not only the
responsibility of our leaders, but of each and every one of us. As J.
Krishnamurti so often said, 'You are the world, and the world is you.'
When the power of humility informs and impels our lives, then perhaps peace will break out across the world."

Roy Whenary
British author, *The Texture Of Being*

"With compassion and a no-nonsense approach, the authors safely
guide the reader through dips and valleys of the healing process until
humility is attained. With humility, we see the limitations of our
thinking and way of life and make another choice. The authors present
a roadmap of healing and wholeness that requires awareness, persist-
ence, knowledge and practical know-how. Humility is the power that
moves us forward into awareness of the Self, and marks a significant
turning point in the soul's development. "

Susan S. Trout, Ph.D.
Author, *The Awakened Leader: Leadership as a Classroom of the Soul*

"Combining truths from multiple respected sources, the authors
show us how to use effective psycho-spiritual principles to help heal
our conflicted and painful relationships. *The Power of Humility* gives
us tools to resolve interpersonal struggles, particularly codependence,
power games and difficult relationships. It combines spiritual and

psychological truths from Buddhism, *A Course in Miracles,* Native American tradition, other Eastern and Western belief systems, and the recovery movement, including the Twelve Steps. This approach to handling conflict is what millions of people in our society have been searching for and have not yet discovered. The four authors have successfully brought their accumulated wisdom together. What a gift for the masses who have needed such guidance, but did not know where to find it."

Judith S. Miller, Ph.D.
Professor of Psychology, Columbia University
Author of *Direct Connection: Transformation of Consciousness*

"Reading *The Power of Humility* has left me with a feeling of peace, and that all is well. I have had the experience of childhood trauma and know what it is like to repeat unhealthy patterns until you take responsibility for your healing and make the connection with your Heart and True Self.

"The triangle levels is powerful information, reminding me that until we make a conscious effort to move on to the freedom of Level 2 we live with the painful conflict of a Level 1 triangle every day in our own head. As someone who moved into spiritual awakening at a young age I also took a 'Spiritual Bypass,' which you explain so well. This term highlighted for me a lesson I have been working on for the past few years—that a certain level of spiritual evolvement doesn't automatically bring on emotional growth. It is a profound part of the journey to finally allow ourselves to be with our feelings, hear our own true voice, and experience a connection with our True Self, Higher Self and Higher Power that feels deeper and more real every day. People will be helped on their life's journey by reading this book."

Dana Mrkich
Internationally known writer, speaker; and radio host,
Sydney, Australia

"Highly recommended. Its clear description of humility's power shows us how to have peace in our home, workplace and world."

Sid Yarbrough, M.D.

Bestselling Author of *Healing the Child Within*

THE POWER OF HUMILITY

Choosing Peace Over Conflict in Relationships

Charles L. Whitfield, M.D.
Barbara H. Whitfield, R.T., C.M.T.
Russell D. Park, Ph.D. & Jeneane Prevatt, Ph.D.

Health Communications, Inc.
Deerfield Beach, Florida

www.bcibooks.com

Library of Congress Cataloging-in-Publication Data
is available from the Library of Congress

©2006 Charles Whitfield, Barbara Whitfield, Russell Park and Jeneane Prevatt
ISBN 0-7573-0399-4

Publisher: Health Communications, Inc.
         3201 S.W. 15th Street
         Deerfield Beach, FL 33442-8190

Cover design by Lawna Patterson Oldfield
Inside book design by Lawna Patterson Oldfield
Inside book formatting by Dawn Von Strolley Grove

This book is dedicated
to all who search for peace in a time of conflict.

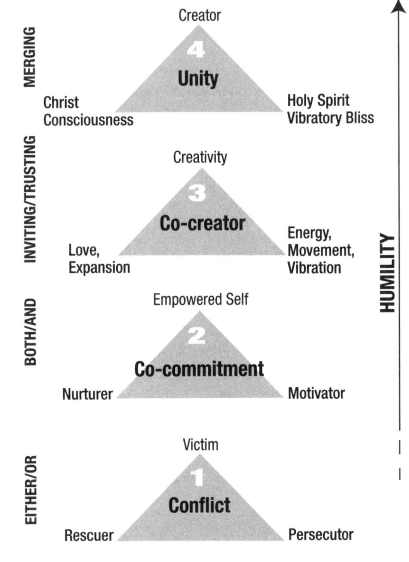

CONTENTS

Histories

Tables

Sidebars

ACKNOWLEDGMENTS

We thank Jyoti and Russ for bringing these concepts to us. In the writing we incorporated them into our own clinical and spiritual experience. Writing this book with them has expanded our understanding and skills for advanced healing and recovery work when people find themselves conflicted and enmeshed in triangles and other painful relationships.

Thanks to Steven Harris, Nicholas Whitfield and Greg Murphy for their contribution, and thank you to Marshall Silverman, Francesca Sorrentino, Kate Hart and Kyle Gies. We also want to thank Robynne Moran for her input and suggestions that made this a better book.

—Charlie and Barbara Whitfield

The triangles presented in this book are not something we developed just in our minds through a conscious, cognitive process. We had taught concepts regarding the first two triangles for a number of years and had shared that knowledge with students. The evolution of that understanding and the other triangles grew out of our dialogue in community. The model we are presenting is a direct result of shared experiences. We want to thank Karen Barsell and Patricia James[1] for helping give form to those experiences. Their inspiration and encouragement gave this project life. And we want to thank Barbara and Charlie for the many hours of exploring and defining that brought this work forward. We each came to the table with different parts of this story, and it is our hope that what resulted from our collaboration will cultivate peace in a time of conflict.

—Jyoti (Jeneane Prevatt) and Russell Park

All four of us also thank Peter Vegso, Amy Hughes and Allison Janse, and the fine staff at Health Communications, for their excellent work in publishing this book.

INTRODUCTION

Humility involves relationships. These include our relationships with ourselves, others and, if we choose, the God of our understanding. We can begin to define humility as *having openness to learning more* about these three relationships. In this book we will explore humility—and how we can use it to our benefit—from the perspective of all three of these relationships.

Humility is not about groveling or being a doormat. Instead, it is a powerful attitude and state of mind that, when we are in the pain of conflict, opens us to more choices and peaceful resolutions. Humility assists our ordinary ego-centered unawareness into a more expansive, alive and conscious awareness.

A useful angle from which we will explore humility will expand the crucial two-way relationships with self, others and God into the common situation when a third member enters, so that our interactions involve three people. Triangles happen often in our everyday life—especially in our family and workplace. The following case history illustrates a workplace triangle solved with the power of humility.

HISTORY I.1: DEAN'S STORY

Dean worked for his software company since its inception. Now only two years later the company has grown to the point where Dean's area of expertise is big enough to have eight employees and become a separate and unique department. It was logical for him to become the head of it. Dean worked on his new position often in his psychotherapy group, which was specifically for adults who had been repeatedly traumatized as children.

"Ever since they put the title of 'head of the department' on me, everything has fallen apart. It's like there are two factions fighting each other, and I usually find myself stuck in the middle. I got more done when I was the only one doing this work." The group repeatedly asked him if this could be related to his dysfunctional family when he was growing up. He came from a family of eight children who, even today, don't communicate with one another. After working on this issue over several group therapy sessions, Dean had an eventual realization that he was replaying the role of rescuer from his family, where he also tried to rescue his siblings whenever there was conflict. He saw himself at work as being the "peacemaker" and was able to reframe that to being the rescuer who eventually became the victim of most of these work colleagues. It was his humility—as opposed to possible denial or arrogance—that allowed him to make these connections.

His therapy group helped him discover that he had more choices, including stepping down as the head of the department and enjoying his work or learning new skills as a leader. In group therapy, he practiced speaking to his department members with humility yet without needing to rescue or triangle with them into individual and three-way conflicts. He developed a new attitude in himself that he says "feels so much better than the way it was before. Before it was my sibs fighting with each other, and my Dad screaming at us to stop, and me trying to hold everyone down and keep things calm."

Through Dean's desire to learn more about himself (humility), his work in group therapy gave him insight about his feelings and actions, helped him reframe his conflicts, change his behavior and attain a more peaceful life.

CHOOSING PEACE OVER CONFLICT IN RELATIONSHIPS

When we have three healthy two-way relationships it is a healthy threesome, which is ideal.[2]

But when a two-way relationship develops its own conflict to such a degree that one or both of its members cannot tolerate its intensity, then one or both of these two who are now conflicted may bring in a third person to try to lessen the pain of their conflict. This is not ideal and leads to what is called *triangling-in* the third person, thus generating what clinicians call a triangle. The third member may also be a place or a thing, as exemplified by the Twelve Step reference to "people, places and things" as sources of conflict.

Paradoxically, triangles tend to generate even more pain for the two original people-in-conflict, so that one or both of these may sooner or later wish that they had never initiated bringing the third aboard.

One healthy and traditional way of getting out of a triangle is to deal directly with the original party by working out our original conflict with that person, while at the same time refusing to participate in the newly generated conflicts that have developed from bringing in a third member. Called *de-triangling*, this method tends to lessen our painful conflicts over time.

THE ROLE OF HUMILITY

Yet triangles often persist and reappear in different guises. We have choices to handle the conflict and pain that we feel when we find ourselves in a triangle. For example, the power of humility (as shown in the preceding history) can be used in the workplace where two or more people have polarized against each other to the detriment of the company's functioning. It can also be used to bring about peace in conflicted families and other painful relationships.

Humility (if found in each individual) can bring the conflicted polarity out of a painful *either/or* stance into a *both/and* reality of co-commitment that will be healing for everyone, including a family, company, organization or group. After describing co-commitment we offer individual and co-creative skills for rising to yet another level in our relationships. Finally, we peek into unity, a level of consciousness once believed to be available to only a few of us. Recent research, however, shows that more of us are naturally touching these high spiritual levels and living to talk about it.[3]

In this book we will offer effective ways that we and others have found for lessening and healing our conflicted and painful relationships and achieving a lasting peace.

PART ONE

INTRODUCING
HUMILITY

Chapter 1

Our Global Story

The pain of unresolved conflict is common. Many of us live with it every day. For example, on 9/11 our prior worldview of the safety within our shores was shattered by fundamentalist religious terrorists. These people are polarized against anyone not like themselves and locked into a primitive view and way of handling conflict. This conflict is a double-edged sword—it both unites us with each other and separates us from them.

How can we best handle this painful time? What possibilities and choices do we have? What are the implications, both personally and collectively, of our choices in creating our future? Could the tragedy of 9/11, in a strange way, be the beginning of a new era?

Perhaps if we each work to heal ourselves, eventually and collectively we can help to heal our world. We start by listening to the conflicts within ourselves. Then we work with others to heal our personal relationships. In this book, we offer new skills for a new way of peaceful being with ourselves, others and the God of our understanding. We take this new knowledge into our lives and world and watch this fresh way of handling conflict develop, evolve and spread.

The following is a history that demonstrates the constructive use of humility in a personal conflict.

HISTORY 1.1: SANDRA'S STORY

Sandra, a fifty-five-year-old "adult child" of an alcoholic has been in recovery for four years. She has three married children and is in a second marriage of ten years. She told her psychotherapy group after she and her husband returned from a ten-day visit with two of her children and their families in another state:

> My husband and I were together constantly for several days and spontaneously started to argue as we walked into my son's house. My grandson and son were standing there, and it was quite embarrassing, but we couldn't stop snapping at each other. After several minutes I said I was going shopping with my grandson, and my husband took off with my son, who said as we were all leaving, "I'm convinced that all couples fight, and it's no big deal."
>
> I could feel my embarrassment fade away, and I started to examine my anger at my husband. I knew we had been together too much or much more than we are used to. I spent the rest of the day with my kids trying to stay away from him but not being obvious. Driving back to our motel, I looked at him and again replayed in my mind what he had said and how he looked when I snapped at him. I remembered our discussions in group about the feelings that are painful boiling up from our unresolved anger from when we were kids. My anger at the moment we snapped at each other was much bigger than what was

going on between us, and it felt like we were both out of control. I felt a tinge of compassion for him. I know his family background and suddenly realized how much pain he must have been in to snap at me like that. In a moment of humility, I made a conscious decision not to focus on my anger and to focus instead on my compassion for him. When we got back to the motel I told him about that, and he then told me why he had snapped at me. It wasn't the mean reason I originally believed, and so I told him why I got angry back. He didn't know I felt that way either. We talked it out, making sure we listened and believed each other's reasons. We ended up embracing and saying how much we love each other and even expressed how we wanted to walk through the rest of this lifetime together.

I think the whole situation turned around for me when my son said, "All couples fight," which removed my embarrassment and got me grounded. He didn't try to rescue us, although I believe his action was the beginning of some motivation to change our bickering into something better. Later, we became empowered instead of rotating the roles of victim and persecutor. It was an important experience of learning not to focus on anger. We have choices now. If we just look carefully at the people we love, we can allow the compassion in our hearts to well up and help us shift away from anger and into something that is so much better for us all.

This is what we call a Level 1 conflict. The use of humility by both members of the conflict allowed them to move from conflict to Level 2 co-commitment, and thereby let go of the tension in the conflict and feel peace.

No matter what kind of conflicts we may have, key to naming and working through them is identifying the potentially useful role of humility. Once identified, we can then use the power of our humility to handle conflicts as they come up for us individually, within our family or workplace, or regionally and globally. In this book we develop the power of humility through its use in the common conflicted relationship of the classical psychological and emotional triangle (which we explain in Chapter 5).

HANDLING CONFLICTS

How can we achieve peace? How can we best handle a personal conflict? A family conflict? A group or a national conflict? One solution is to cultivate an attitude that allows us to develop what psychologist Arthur Deikman and others call our nonjudgmental *observer self*[4] (also called our *Sacred Witness*). By doing so we can thereby raise our thinking and functioning to higher and more efficient levels. These conflicts then become challenges. Some of these challenges include: our unconscious conflicts (including the effects of trauma), addictions, cultural prejudices, family dysfunctions, cultural and community breakdowns, competitive survival and coping patterns, defensive and territorial posturing, and ultimately, personal and group spiritual crisis. These and other core issues commonly reflect some of our unresolved conflicts that keep us in *chronic stress* and *distress,* and thereby stuck in what we call the first, or Level 1 triangle.

If we can cultivate our personal and collective or global observer self/Sacred Witness, we can embrace our individual and group preferences and uniqueness, cooperating rather than competing with each other, and developing an attitude of inclusion instead of exclusion, self instead of ego, soul instead of personality, and "we" instead of just "I." Through this shift in identity, we begin to empower an attitude of unity through diversity.

As individual and group growth and personal spirituality emerges, one component is community. Community can act as a container that allows us to freely share our view of a conflict—of what is challenging us. If we can learn not only to "actively listen" to each other, but to hold "divine respect" for each member, we can begin to see more options to handle a conflict.

In this book, we will give examples of handling conflict from several perspectives, including (1) cross-cultural or anthropological, (2) relationship or system dynamics, (3) some clinical histories, and from (4) spirituality. Thus, we lift ourselves out of Level 1 triangles into new and progressively more expanded and peaceful levels. Using triangle dynamics we will propose three more levels of functioning: Level 2, Level 3 and Level 4 (see Table 1.1). In Part Two of this book, we describe the most conflicted and Level 1 triangles in some detail because they are the most difficult and painful. Then, in Part Three, we describe and discuss the expanded more peaceful levels of functioning and being.

DIFFERENT WORLD VIEWS

For an example from a cross-cultural view, we can look at levels of consciousness described in some Eastern medical and

Table 1.1 Defining Some Clinical Therapeutic Properties of the Chakras: With Emphasis on the Self
(Chakras 1 Through 7)

TRIANGLE LEVEL	CHAKRA (Level of Consciousness)	LOVE	TRUTH	HEALING	POWER
FOUR	7) Unity Consciousness	Peaceful Being			
THREE	6) Compassion	Unconditional Empathy and Acceptance		Love and Acceptance	
	5) Understanding Growth	Commitment to Growth	Creativity	Right Decision	Wisdom
TWO	4) Acceptance/Heart	Experience, Acceptance and Forgiveness			
ONE	3) Mind/Ego	Worship, Possession	Experience, Beliefs	Prevention, Education Psychological	Assertion, Persuasion
	2) Passion	"Chemistry"	Sensations	Nurturance	Manipulation
	1) Survival	Neediness	Science	Physical	Physical Strength

Source: Expanded from Whitfield C. L., 1985

religious models. These levels or energy centers are called *chakras* in Sanskrit, which means *wheel* and describes energy centers or transducers that convey energy from one dimension into another. Each chakra is located in the energy body of each of us and mediates a different level of consciousness with the outer environment (see Figure 1.1). The first chakra, at the base of the spine, mediates survival. The second chakra, at the level of the navel, is passion. The third chakra, at the level of the diaphragm, mediates mind/ego. The fourth chakra, at the heart level, is acceptance/heart issues. The fifth chakra, at the throat, is a synthesis of head and heart and mediates understanding. The sixth chakra, between our eyebrows, mediates compassion. The seventh chakra, at the top of the head, funnels unlimited spiritual energy in and mediates Unity Consciousness.

Figure 1.1 Schematic of the Seven Chakras

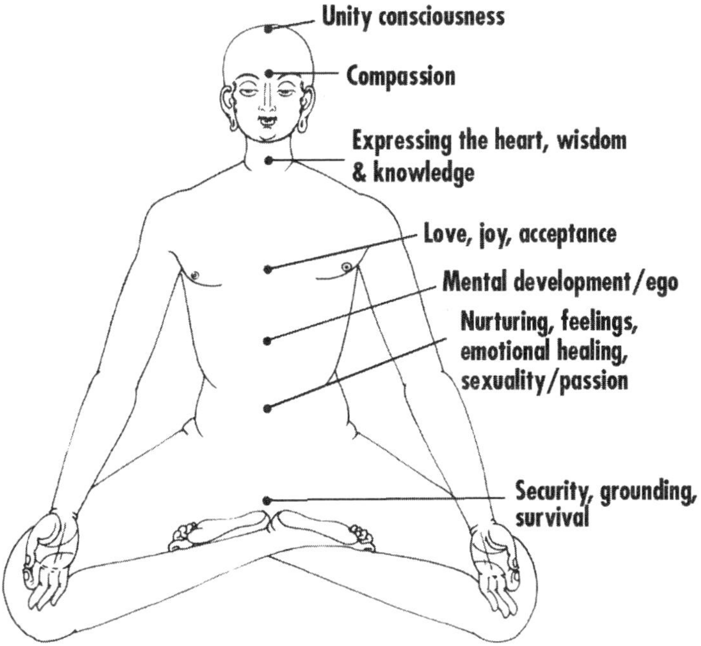

Unity consciousness

Compassion

Expressing the heart, wisdom & knowledge

Love, joy, acceptance

Mental development/ego

Nurturing, feelings, emotional healing, sexuality/passion

Security, grounding, survival

Related to the chakras is the idea that the earth is evolving in yet another way: from an ego-bound (third chakra) position to a heartfelt (fourth chakra) sense of awareness. In other words, we are moving from struggles with survival, control and power to issues of the heart: power over others versus empowerment within ourselves. At the heart level we begin to see our glass as being half-full instead of half-empty, to see our conflicts and styles as co-creative stimuli rather than polarized posturing, and to know ourselves and the power of our choices rather than feeling victimized by our situations. We can thereby begin to feel our stress decreasing. We can start to see our conflicts and crises as opportunity.

ANOTHER CROSS-CULTURAL EXAMPLE

The Hopi Indians model a community that takes the time to weigh out each important decision that they make in accordance with how it may impact the next seven generations.[5] The Hopi seem to understand and experience the interrelationship of all creation. Can we take time to learn—as these and other indigenous peoples do—from our elders and from our children? With humility, the Hopi recognize children and elders as being the ones who are closest to God, thereby honoring their wisdom and guidance.

As we begin to integrate this attitude of natural spirituality into our everyday lives, our awareness and consciousness expands, allowing us to experience our abundance and move out of scarcity thinking or never having "enough." We begin to see possibilities revealing themselves, and a new worldview or myth unfolding. "Problems" become simply "situations," and now we are open to new choices. We begin to identify with our "goodness" rather than our conflicts. Synchronicities (meaningful coincidences) and at times miracles (unexplained positive events), can take their natural place in our lives.

If we are about to go into a new world personally, nationally and globally with multidimensional implications, what will be the result of our choices? Consider looking at your daily activities. What choices have you made? Are there incongruities in what you say you are and how you live? Are you walking your talk?

Psychologist Carl Jung said that we are living in a time when the worldviews (archetypes) are shifting and that the most difficult times would be when the old worldviews leave center stage and the new have not yet revealed themselves. Our great challenge will be to relate from our hearts, having compassion for each other, as we birth a new era and leave a living legacy for our children.

Can we be mindful of our next seven generations? The Hopi Elders prophecy can guide us:

We Are the Ones We Have Been Waiting For [6]

You have been telling the people that this is the eleventh Hour.

Now return and tell them the Hour has come, and they must now consider:

Where are you living?

What are you doing?

What are your relationships? Are they right relationships?

Where is your water?

Know your Garden.

It is time to speak your Truth.

Create your community.

Be good to each other.

And do not look outside yourself for the Leader.

This could be a good time!

The river now flows very fast, so great and swift that some will be afraid, and will suffer much. Know the river has a destination. We must now let go of the shore, push off into the middle, keeping our eyes open and our heads above water. And see who is there with you, and celebrate! At this point in our history, we must take nothing personally, least of all ourselves.

For, in the instant we do, our spiritual journey comes to a halt.

The Lone Wolf's time is over. Gather yourselves! All we do must be done in a sacred manner and in celebration.

We are the ones we've been waiting for.

Hopi Nation Elders
Oraibi, Arizona, 2000

We believe that this is not a goal to leave just for our politicians and other authority figures (who we know are often inconsistent and unconstructive in their actions). The Hopi elders concluded, "We are the ones we've been waiting for." We start within ourselves. We take our conflicting thoughts and move them up—eventually to peace. We touch others with this action—the empowerment of our own humility. And then, hopefully, it spreads to include our political system, and then it moves out and spreads to include everyone on the planet.

<hr />

At the beginning of this chapter we said that a key factor in working through our conflicts is identifying the potentially useful role of humility in each of them. In the next chapter we will describe some of the important characteristics of humility.

Chapter 2

Humility

Taken from its origin *humus,* meaning *earthly,* the general dictionary definition of humble is twofold: (1) not proud or arrogant; modest; and (2) meek; submissive; low in rank or conditions.[7] It is in part on this first definition that we have focused and expanded.

CHARACTERISTICS OF HUMILITY

We believe there are at least twelve key characteristics of humility. These include (1) openness, (2) an attitude of "don't know," (3) curiosity, (4) innocence, (5) a childlike nature, (6) spontaneity, (7) spirituality, (8) tolerance, (9) patience, (10) integrity, (11) detachment and (12) letting go—all of which lead to inner peace. Like the hours on a clock, each of these is an important part of the power of humility (see Figure 2.1).

Figure 2.1

Clock Diagram of Humility

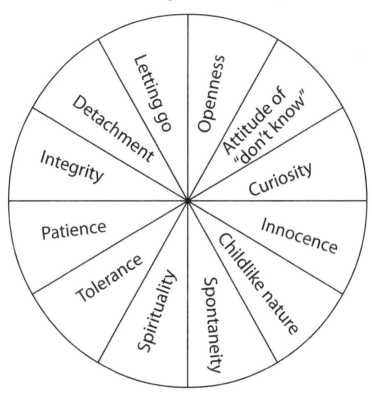

Openness

Early in this book we began to define humility as being open to learning more about ourselves, others and God. This openness is perhaps its most basic and key characteristic. Without being open to what *is* we may miss countless chances to learn, experience and grow. When we have humility there is no such thing as failure. Each act or experience has something to teach us, even if it doesn't turn out the way we planned.

"Don't Know"

The Third Chinese Patriarch of Zen, Seng Ts'an, wrote: "The Great Way is not difficult for those who have no preferences. When love and hate are both absent, everything becomes clear and undisguised. Make the smallest distinction, however, and heaven and earth are set infinitely apart. If you wish to see the truth, then hold no opinions for or against anything."[8]

Having an attitude of not knowing the answer to every question or conflict we encounter gives us the chance to let go of always needing to come up with an answer or even be right, which may block our ability to experience inner peace and serenity. This "don't know" stance is a basic and effective tenet of Buddhist philosophy and practice. By not knowing, we expand our possibilities. We don't limit ourselves. And we thereby have a greater chance to avoid conflict in or outside of triangles.

A Course in Miracles says: "Let us be still an instant, and forget all things we ever learned, all thoughts we had and every preconception that we hold of what things mean and what their purpose is. Let us remember not our own ideas of what the world is for. We do not know. Let every image held of everyone be loosened from our minds and swept away." It continues, "Be innocent of judgment, unaware of any thoughts of evil or of good that ever crossed your mind of anything."[9]

Curiosity

Have you ever thought you already knew the truth about someone or something and found out later that you were wrong? Having humility, including openness to learning more, an attitude of "don't know," and being curious about people, places and things, can help us to work through conflicts, including when we find ourselves caught in the pain of a Level 1 triangle. Curiosity drives us to see the authenticity of other people. Instead of the old habit from Level 1 of projecting onto others our conflicts and other unfinished business, our curiosity opens us to acceptance instead of prejudice and rejection.

Innocence

As we look at newborn infants we are reminded that we are innocent at our core. If God made us, and we are each a part of God, how can we also be sinners (as some religions claim)? *A Course in Miracles* suggests that we are not. Rather than being born in "original sin," the Course says that we are born innocent. We are already and eternally innocent.

While the Course describes various aspects of innocence, it defines it as being the same as having Christ's vision, which it also calls *true perception* and *right-mindedness*. Innocence means that we never see what does not exist (that is, the ego and its world) and always see what does (God and God's real world). At the core of our being, what we are innocent about or unaware of is our ego and its world of pain.

After reading parts of the Course, we (BW and CW) realized that upon entering the dream of the ego's world, we unknowingly caused our own pain. We were and are innocent, and were simply in a dream. The lion and the lamb lying down together symbolize that strength and innocence are not in conflict, but naturally live in peace. A pure mind knows that innocence is strength. We enter into our innocence each time that we co-create peace with another with whom we may be in conflict.

Childlike

The Romantic poets, especially William Blake, spoke often of our innocence. In his long poem "Songs of Innocence and Experience," Blake said that we are innocent and that we can contact our innocence through the child within us. In workbook lesson 182 the Course says ". . . there is a Child in you who seeks his Father's house. . . . This childhood is eternal, with an innocence that will endure forever."[10] To us, this is one of the most moving of the Course's 365 workbook lessons.

The Course says that whenever we are in conflict we are in our ego, projecting sin, guilt and shame onto the person(s) with whom we are in conflict. If we see sin and badness in another we lose the peace of our innocence. If we see any error in them and attack them for it, we hurt ourselves.[11] It says that "You cannot know your brother when you attack him. . . . You are making him a stranger by misperceiving him, and so you cannot know him."[12]

Spontaneity

Being spontaneous means living as our real selves in this moment of now. Our True Self exists only in the eternal now. As soon as we honor the present moment, all unhappiness and struggle dissolve, and life begins to flow with more ease and joy. Every time we let ourselves go into the past (usually from guilt or shame) or project into the future (usually from fear), we are energizing our ego, which usually causes us conflict and pain. We know we are in our ego when we are not at peace. In our True Self we not only experience stillness and peace, but also joy and intense aliveness.[13]

Spirituality

Spirituality is about our relationship with self, others and the God of our understanding. And it is much more. Whereas religion takes us by the hand—and we follow the usually preordained path of those who have gone before us—spirituality is about our own personal path. We do it our own way and in our own time. We form an experiential bond with self, others and God that we may or may not find in religion.

By breaking new ground our journey becomes our goal. This is what the Course calls "The Journey without Distance." It says: "The Journey to God is merely the reawakening of the Knowledge of where you are always, and what you are forever. It is a journey without distance to a goal that has never changed."[14]

Our goal in living our journey is to surrender, including surrendering to the moment we are in. Surrender is not weakness. It is strength. A person who has surrendered has spiritual power. In this surrender, there are no longer problems; there are only situations. And if we don't like the situation we can choose again.[15] As part of humility, spirituality leads to detaching from or letting go of our numerous attachments, resulting in inner peace.

Tolerance

Tolerance involves the capacity for or the practice of recognizing and respecting the beliefs, preferences or practices of ourselves, others and God. The Buddhist teacher Cheri Huber says, "Suffering is resisting what is."

If a situation is intolerable and we suffer from it, we have three options: (1) remove ourselves from the situation, (2) change it or (3) accept it as it is.[16] We can be *pushed* by our pain and suffering or *pulled* by our spiritual vision.

Patience

Patience may be one of our hardest lessons to attain. When we are in our ego, we want everything *right now*. Our ego has no patience and as such may lead us to believe we are being mistreated, empty, bored or otherwise in pain. It's almost humorous to realize the spectrum of emotions we experience when we find ourselves stuck in our ego. All we need do is slide over to patience and, if we struggle with patience, practice tolerance in our struggle.

An effective way out of pain from being in conflict with a person, place or thing is to use prayer. When we are not at peace, we can remember that we are in our ego. In our prayer we simply ask for help and then surrender to the God of our understanding. On a humorous note, we can consider the prayer for patience: "Lord give me patience, and give it to me *now!*"

Integrity

Humility breeds integrity and vice versa. They support and feed one another in a positive way. Integrity means wholeness. Integrity is one of the most important and oft-cited of virtue terms. It is also puzzling. For example, while it is sometimes used instead of "moral," we also at times distinguish acting morally from acting with integrity. We believe that humility leads to integrity. And people with true integrity have humility at their base and actions.

What a conflicted world may need now is integrity—in ourselves, in our relationships, and in our private and political systems. The more we incorporate humility in our interaction and intra-actions (that is, our inner life), the more we move up the Four Levels that we describe in this book, and the more integrity becomes an active part of our being. Why? Because integrity means we are whole, we are working from our authentic selves, who God made us to be, and at the same time we are wholly taking in the people and the world around us.

Detachment

Detachment involves withdrawing our emotional attachment to a person, place, thing or outcome of any situation—including our conflicts. It involves releasing our attachment or connection. Detachment is sometimes mistakenly interpreted to mean "to not care about," but the word actually means "to separate from." It requires a willingness to let go and allow others to take responsibility for their own lives. This is especially difficult for the "rescuer" in a Level 1 triangle (explained in Chapter 4), who feels driven to jump in and help or "fix" the "victim's" plight. If rescuers do not learn to detach, they often become the victims.

Detachment is a keystone skill in recovery for members of the Twelve Step fellowship of Al-Anon. Many of the principles of Buddhism and related paths illustrate similarities with Al-Anon's view of detachment. The Four Noble Truths of Buddhism include:

1. Life involves suffering.
2. Attachment, desire, selfish craving or clinging of our ego causes our suffering.
3. Detachment is the cure for suffering.
4. Detachment can follow an eightfold path.[17]

This eightfold path includes right association (that is, with people who have positive attitudes and clarity). It also involves several key principles and spiritual practices that embrace integrity and meditation.[18]

Figure 2.2

Some Components and Practices of Detachment

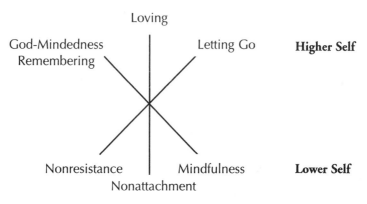

Source: Modified from Naranjo, 1983; *The One Quest*

The eightfold path of Buddhism includes right: (1) knowledge (learning the truths and the path), (2) aspiration, (3) speech (language, honesty, clarity and positivity), (4) behavior, (5) livelihood, (6) effort, (7) mindfulness and (8) meditation.

In summary, expanding upon the work of Naranjo, we see at least six principle features of detachment. From a lower-self perspective, these include nonresistance, nonattachment and mindfulness. From a higher-self perspective, these include God-mindedness and remembering, loving, and letting go (see Figure 2.2).

Letting Go

Letting go is both an inner life process and an event. When we can remember, it is also often a series of continuous events. We work in our recovery process to let go of our accumulated baggage from past traumas, including how our ego has beaten us up. Letting go is in large part about letting go of our ego. When we let go of our ego, being humble becomes easier.

When we are whole, when we are living as our True Self, we can help the people we love by being present with them and loving them unconditionally. But we can't fix anyone. We surrender our ego's need to control this reality that we share with our loved ones and move into the larger reality, where our inner life and the light of unconditional love work together. As we move into balance, our relationships move into balance.

As we give everyone around us the space to be who they are, which also involves unconditional love, we give ourselves the same space. One of the rules of the Universe becomes so obvious: We treat others as we want to be treated, and then everything we give out comes back.

BEING HUMBLE

Having summarized the twelve characteristics of being humble, we will now describe some further principles of humility in recovery and in life. Gaining humility is a major milestone in recovery. It usually signifies a life transformation in that the person flows more with life, functions better, and tends to be at a lower risk of falling back into Level 1 functioning and pain. For all concerned, being "humble" is thus positive and a great strength; it is not a weakness.

Gratitude

As we let go and watch our relationships transform, transcend or dissolve, we not only recognize all the characteristics of humility playing out in us and our loved ones—gratitude moves in and possibly even takes over as an underlying continual attitude or mood.

When the stressful pressure of conflicted and painful relationships is released, something needs to take its place. (The Universe seems to fill in a vacuum.) And that something is peace and gratitude. We feel better. Our ego isn't running our inner life anymore. Our inner life now involves more of our Sacred Person (see map of the mind on page 39).

Being "Nobody Special"

Writer Roy Whenary puts it this way: "The story of life, of humanity, of the universe, is vast in terms of what we know, or what we can ever understand. Death comes, like birth, and there is nothing we can do about it. Strutting and fretting our brief hour upon the stage of life is really quite meaningless. In stepping back and seeing the play from the perspective of one's true nature, compassion arises for all. Humility becomes one's natural clothing. There is no one, no person, no doer, no diver, yet all is blissful when the mind with all its knowledge, memory and emotional residues stands back and lets go of its hold on life."[19]

In the process of humility we work through a cycle early in

our lives from becoming ego-attached or "somebody special," to then becoming ego-detached or "nobody special." In *Grist for the Mill,* spiritual teachers Ram Dass and Stephen Levine says:

> We are in training to be nobody special. It is in that nobody-specialness that we can be anybody. The fatigue, the neurosis, the anxiety, the fear, all come from identifying with the somebody-ness. But you have to start somewhere. It does seem that you have to be somebody before you can be nobody. If you started out being nobody at the beginning of this incarnation, you probably wouldn't have made it this far. . . . It's that force of somebody-ness that develops the social and physical survival mechanisms. It's only now, having evolved to this point that we learn to put that somebody-ness, that whole survival kit, which we called the ego, into perspective.
>
> At first you really "think" you've lost something. It's a while before you can appreciate the peace that comes from the simplicity of no-mind, of just emptiness, of not having to be somebody all the time. . . . You spent the first half of your life becoming somebody. Now you can work on becoming nobody, which is really somebody. For when you become nobody there is no tension, no pretense, no one trying to be anyone or anything, and the natural state of the mind shines through unobstructed—the natural state of the mind is pure love . . . pure awareness. Can you imagine when you become that place you've only touched through your meditations? . . . You've cleared away all of the mind trips that kept you being who you thought you were. . . . You experience the exquisiteness of being in love with everybody and not

having to do anything about it. Because you've developed compassion. The compassion is to let people be as they need to be without coming on to them. The only time you come on to people is when their actions are limiting the opportunities for other human beings to be free."[20]

In a society where everybody has to be somebody special, what a joy it can be to walk along and be nobody special. It is freeing, peaceful and serene. We learn to listen and hear. And where we are when we are nobody special is in the heart of our True Self. Our True Self is energized when we are no longer using our energy to be special.

Twelve Step fellowships also suggest being nobody special by their principle of anonymity. Their Twelfth Tradition says, "Anonymity is the spiritual foundation of our Traditions, ever reminding us to place principles before personalities."

At the beginning of this chapter we noted twelve key characteristics of humility. Most of these are important components in the process of becoming and being nobody special, which is also a hallmark of humility.

CONCLUSION

We summarize these 12 characteristics of humility, plus its two additional dimensions of gratitude and being "nobody special" in table 2.3. Developing these takes patience and persistance throughout our recovery and life.

Table 2.1 Characteristics of Humility

Characteristic	Description
Openness	Basic and key to feel peace
Attitude of "don't know"	Two "quote" examples: Third Zen Patriarch & ACIM
Curiosity	Awareness, openness & willingness
Innocence	Child of God, true perception, right mindedness
A child-like nature	William Blake's Innocence, ACIM quotes
Spontaneity	Living as Real Self now, not as ego
Spirituality	Awareness of relationship wipth self, others and God
Tolerance	Respecting others, accepting what is
Patience	ego v. letting go
Integrity	In alignment with True Self
Detachment	Letting go with love and compassion (see Fig. 2.1 Eightfold path) Inner and outer process.
Letting go	Inner process and event
Gratitude	Thankfulness spilling over
Being "nobody special"	Whenary & Ram Dass Quotes

In the next chapter we look at three stories—two with humility and one without it.

Chapter 3

Humility:
With or Without It

Growing humility—the power of "don't know"—allows others to be themselves around us. Without our judging or taking their inventory, they feel safe. Our humility allows for different interpretations of the same event. It allows us to reframe our point of view. Not attached to being "right" or "wrong," we are more inclusive of others and don't compete with their reality. We cultivate a sense of "unity in diversity," rather than a need to compete or compare. When we explore what we "don't know," we invite experiences into our lives that our ego didn't plan, expect or imagine. We make a place for mystery, possibility and peace in our lives. We develop trust by being honest with ourselves and others regarding our inner life.

PARADOX

The higher we move up the levels, the more we encounter paradox. And depending on how we respond—the closer we get to God. Considering and addressing paradox teaches us about conflict. This is because paradox offers us different perspectives and levels and ultimately speaks to knowing more about the whole of a process. The poet Rainer Maria Rilke said, "Take your well-disciplined strength and stretch it between two opposing poles, for inside human beings is where God learns." If we learn to hold the tension of such a moment, a third unknown outcome may present itself.

Rumi, the thirteenth-century Persian poet, said, "Beyond ideas of right doing and wrong doing, there is a field. I will meet you there." Thus, if we can hold the paradox of any moment, within conflict, we may discover a new self-awareness that brings us new possibilities and choices. If we apply this powerful potential to our lives, we arrive at our heart. Once we have learned to incorporate this new openness and possibility, our field of choices expands, and then we can teach our ego not to be overwhelmed. We learn how to balance our lives in the vision that pulls us toward our Real Self and into the advantages of Levels 2 and 3. We make our choices by embracing them with an *inclusive* attitude of both/and instead of either/or. We say "yes." As our capacity to be with our life increases, so does our level of tolerance and balance. The dynamic process that fuels our development seeks our deeper nature. The energy of our being begins to manifest in our waking life. Life becomes a kind of meditation practice and our Higher Self becomes visible in our daily activity.

HISTORY 3.1: ROSE'S STORY

I (RP) worked with a woman for about six months who was having relationship problems with her adult son. She was not able to talk to him after a family situation had triggered her, and he in turn raged at her. If she had tried to resolve that with him when he was raging six months earlier, she would have been in a Level 1 triangle with him.

There was a situation that arose during a holiday family dinner between her ex-husband (her son's father) and herself. They were both in Level 1. Rose perceived that she was the victim and he was the persecutor. And her son thought the opposite. She tried to talk about it with her son when they were alone, but he started raging, and she believed he was rescuing his father by attacking her. That's how it started, and she realized at that moment that she was powerless. She came to me for help. She said that she didn't engage her son in his attack because she knew she would be feeding both of their egos (in a Level 1 triangle, described on page 49 and following pages). For six months she processed and prayed over this painful situation. She was learning how to hold and tolerate her emotional pain.

Finally she sat down with him. The first thing she did was tell him that she had realized that from his perspective he was right and she was wrong. She could honor that. This began to pull them out of Level 1. Then she was able to say, "But I couldn't handle the way you attacked me. I'm getting too sensitive for that. You can tell me things, but don't attack me by yelling or threatening me." And, with an attitude and tone of humility, he said he understood.

She realized that all the rage and other pain she still felt toward her ex-husband had simmered down by giving it six months. If she had reacted in the moment, her toxic feelings would have spread onto and hurt her son more. She could now sit with the son she loved and talk with him. He apologized for the way he had acted.

This story is about choosing not to play the game of life in the first triangle, but waiting until the rage is down and the love is up. When Rose finally thought she had a handle on it, she could work through this issue in a Level 2 triangle (described on page 97 and following pages). She and her son transitioned from unconscious behavior to conscious behavior, and from arrogance and victimhood to humility and gratitude. In the six months of her recovery work, including our weekly psychotherapy sessions, she learned a lot about rage. Rage is an intolerance for the pain of being in conflict to the extent of either raising the voice while expressing extreme anger or just leaving or dissociating whenever there is a conflict. By learning to sit with and hold her emotional pain she was able to increase her awareness to the point of letting go of her need to be right.

CAUTION ABOUT JUDGING OURSELVES AND OTHERS

Knowing that our life is developmental, we can give ourselves a break. Even our triangle model could be used mistakenly for judging others. "*You* are in triangle number 1!"

We have to watch ourselves around that. I (RP) caught myself getting down on myself one day for not being aware, not being conscious of something. I was judging myself for being in a lower triangle. I realized that it was like making judgments of myself for not being able to tie my shoe when I was two years old from a seven-year-old perspective. Tying one's shoe is a developmental task—you can't do it at two—as all of life is, so it is *not* going to help us to make those kinds of judgments. Judgments shut us down and make us feel unsafe. What helps is to accept our limitations (humility), open our awareness and become more conscious—and that will change our behavior, not creating self-hatred because "I can't tie my shoes yet."

The question I like to ask myself is, "Is it conscious or unconscious?" If it's conscious, then I can participate. If it's unconscious, then I need to be aware of how I'm participating. In this strange game of life, nobody is wrong. We are either conscious or not conscious. And we can't make other people conscious.

HISTORY 3.2: STEVE'S STORY
AN ILLUSTRATION OF A HEALTHY THREESOME

This story clearly illustrates what can happen in the workplace if there are three people functioning with humility. It also demonstrates how trust is earned over time.

Four months ago, I began a position as the fine arts director at a private school where I work closely with two women. We had recognized early on that we were a good team. We complemented one another. We had planned and performed several productions and were planning several more. We often confided our feelings and frustrations to one another.

At a department meeting, Sharon, one of my fellow music teachers, shared her frustrations with me. I remained silent, but inwardly I was thinking that some of those feelings were unfounded and that I knew ways to fix those situations for her. Later that same day, I noticed Sharon was missing at the beginning of one of her classes and there was a group of parents of potential students touring the school. Since the parent group was headed for her classroom, I stood in her place at her door to show that her class was supervised. After the group left, she was still absent, so I started her class in an activity. After several minutes, Sharon arrived and I left the class to her. (I did not know that Sharon, who was pregnant at the time, had become suddenly ill and had had to step out.)

I did not say anything to her that day, but later that evening began to think that I should send Sharon an e-mail to address some of her frustrations as well as her class absence. After all, I thought, I had been teaching for ten years longer than she and should step in as her director. I wrote the e-mail, alluding to making more effective use of class time and giving some other advice. As I began writing, a still, small voice inside told me not to write it. I ignored it. My wife told me not to send it, and I ignored her, too.

The next day, Sharon and I were working together with high school musicians. She was friendly and composed. I figured she had read the e-mail, realized that I was right and was starting the day a little wiser. The day went fine.

The following day, Sharon asked me if we could have a meet-ing and bring in Peg, who was the third teacher on our team. At that meeting, I began with a "business as usual" approach and went through some items of creating a unified vision for our department. When I finished I invited Sharon to speak her mind, as she was the one who had initiated the meeting. Sharon said that the e-mail, about which I had mostly forgotten, had hurt her deeply and that she had been unable to sleep because of it. She felt accused of laziness and unprofessional behavior. What I had written made assumptions about her that were unfounded and untrue. After initially attempting a weak defense that she had misunderstood what I had written, I realized that Sharon was right. I had subtly insinuated all of those things. At that moment I knew that the only thing I could do was to acknowledge that I had wronged her and to ask for her forgiveness. She immediately and wholeheartedly forgave me. I was humbled.

A few months later, Steve told us that the bond among the three of them had strengthened and that they all three now trusted one another to act in the best interest of their students as well as themselves.

HISTORY 3.3: A PRISONER'S STORY

While co-teaching a class on Spirituality in Recovery at Rutgers University's Institute on Alcohol and Drug Studies, we (BW and CW) were moved when one of our students told us of his experience. He worked as a counselor at a state prison.

He said that occasionally an inmate will walk around with a Bible and use it as a way to deflect any opportunity for personal growth. They call themselves "born again" and claim (including to the parole board) that they have been healed and that they are now ready to go back out into the public domain. As an example, he told us about a man who had been incarcerated for sexually abusing several of his daughters and his daughters' friends. This counselor had approached the prisoner many times to come into counseling. One day the man announced he had a spiritual experience and requested to see a specific minister who immediately validated his spiritual experience and spontaneous healing. To add to the counselor's shock, the minister requested and led a family session where the convicted pedophile asked his daughters for their forgiveness. And the minister insisted that they forgive him.

We and our other students were sickened. Not only was the convicted pedophile doing a spiritual bypass, but both he and the minister appeared to have had no humility. With the slightest bit of empathy (a trait of humility) they would have never forced these girls—who were already traumatized—into another painful, traumatic experience. With the minister's denying and enabling support, there was no way the counselor or anyone else could help this child molester begin to heal.

In the next chapter we briefly describe a map of the psyche, and an overview of the process of recovery.

Chapter 4

Who Am I?
A Map of the Mind

Throughout the struggle of our human condition, many have asked important questions: Who am I? What am I doing here? Where am I going? How can I get any peace? While the answers to these questions remain a Divine Mystery, we have found it useful to construct a map of the mind or psyche (Figure 4.1). And while the map is not the territory, maps can be useful.

Figure 4.1 Map of the Mind

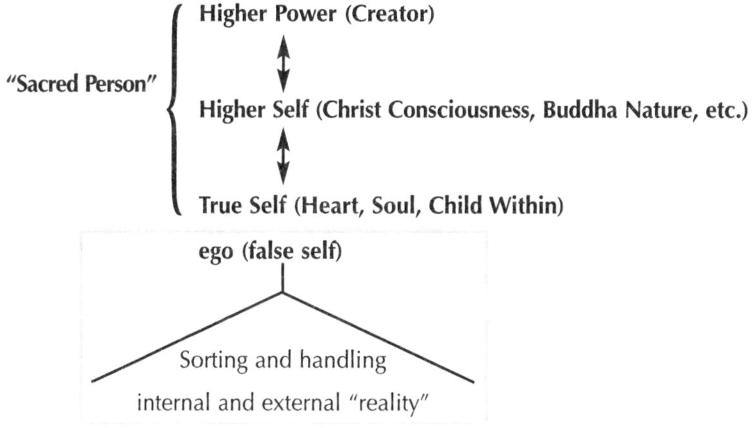

Other names for the True Self—who we really are—include the real or existential self, the human heart, the soul, chakras 4

and 5, and the Child Within. They are all the same because they all refer to our true identity. We also have within us a divine nature, sometimes called a guardian angel, Atman, Buddha Nature, Christ Consciousness, chakras 6 and 7, Higher Self or simply Self. And both of these, our True Self and our Higher Self, are intimately connected to our Higher Power, God/Goddess/ All-That-Is, a part of which is also within us.

We call this important relationship—True Self, Higher Self and Higher Power—for want of a better term, the *Sacred Person*. In a loving, supporting and teaching way, pervading the Sacred Person is the Holy Spirit (Kundalini, Chi, Ki or Divine Energy).

As part of the Mystery, our True Self makes or constructs an assistant to aid us, although in limited ways, as we live out this human experience. We can call this assistant, this sidekick, the ego—also known as the false self or co-dependent self. When this ego is helpful to us, such as in screening, sorting and handling many aspects of our internal and external reality, we can call it positive ego. But when it tries to take over and run our lives, it becomes a negative ego by causing us unnecessary pain.

This map of the psyche is more evolved than those of Freud, Jung and their colleagues of up to one hundred years ago, when they used the term ego to mean both True Self *and* false self. Since the 1930s we have begun to make this more precise differentiation between True Self and false self, and today we see ego as the same as the false self.

The contemporary holy book *A Course in Miracles* says in its introduction:

What is real cannot be threatened.
What is unreal does not exist.
Herein lies the peace of God.

What is real is God and God's world, that of the Sacred Person. The ego and its world are not real, and therefore, in the grand scheme of the Mystery, do not exist. Herein, when we make this differentiation, lies our peace and serenity. When we are humble, that is, when we open ourselves to learning more about self, others and God, we open ourselves up to the world and peace of God.

But growing up in a dysfunctional family and dysfunctional society and world, we may have become significantly hurt or wounded. That wounding made our Child Within, our True Self, go into hiding, and the only one left to run the show was our ego. And because the ego is not competent to run our lives, we often end up feeling confused and hurt.

The way out is to begin to differentiate between identifying with our True Self and our false self, and to heal our wounds around all the past traumas that may have hurt and confused us. While all of this information is useful to know on a cognitive level, it is *healing* only on an experiential level. To heal, we have to *experience* working through our pain as well as living and enjoying our lives.

THE RECOVERY MOVEMENT

Over the decade of the 1980s and through the 1990s, an increasing number of people began awakening to their traumatic experiences and began to heal themselves. This phenomenon, called the recovery movement, is part of a new paradigm, a new and expanded understanding and belief about the recurringly painful part of the human condition and how to heal it. This approach is so effective and has developed so much momentum for so many people for two reasons: It is *grass roots,* that is, its energy comes from the recovering people themselves, and it employs the most accurate and healing of all our accumulated knowledge about the human condition. What is different about this knowledge is that it is now *simplified* and *demystified.*[21]

STAGES OF RECOVERY

Understanding the stages of recovery is important in helping us heal. These are summarized in Table 4.1 and further explained in the sections that follow.

Stage Zero

Stage Zero is manifested by the presence of an active illness or disorder such as an addiction, compulsion or another disorder, including any physical illness. This active illness may be acute, recurring or chronic. Without recovery, it may continue indefinitely. At Stage Zero, recovery has not yet started.

Table 4.1 Recovery and Duration According to Stages

Recovery Stage	Condition	Focus of Recovery	Approximate Duration
3	Human/ Spiritual	Spiritual	Ongoing
2	Past Trauma	Trauma-specific	3 to 5+ years
1	Stage 0 Disorder	Basic-illness full recovery program	6 months to 3 years
0	Active Illness	Usually none	Indefinite

Stage One

Stage One is when recovery begins. It involves participating in a full recovery program to assist in healing the Stage Zero problem, disorder, condition or conditions. A person may have a spiritual awakening while in Stage Zero or Stage One and try to bypass doing Stage Two recovery work (see sidebar, "Spiritual Bypass").

Stage Two

Stage Two is one that many people may try to bypass. It involves healing the effects of past traumas, sometimes called *adult child* or *co-dependence* issues. Once a person has a stable and solid Stage One recovery—one that has lasted for at least a year or longer—it may be time to consider looking into these issues. In this context, an *adult child* is anyone who grew up in an unhealthy, troubled or dysfunctional family. Many such adult children of trauma may still be in a similar unhealthy environment, whether at home, in one or more relationships, or at work.

Stage Three

Stage Three recovery is the one into which we may be compelled prematurely by having a spiritual awakening (a direct experience of Higher Power for a short time). Stage Three is the experience of natural spirituality *and* its incorporation into our daily life by feeling a deepening connection to our Higher Self and Higher Power. This process is ongoing.

If we try to bypass the darkness of our lives to get to the light, that is, if we try to ignore the lower to get to the higher levels of our consciousness, something—we can call it our *shadow* (Jung) or *repetition compulsion* (Freud)—will pull us back until we work through our particular unfinished business. Much of this book is about Stage Three.

Spiritual Bypass

One of the biggest problems at the early stages of the recovery or transformational process is *ego inflation.* Many hear about, read or study the Eastern spiritual literature and may identify strongly with the teachers, gurus or authors. But being Westerners, it may be hard to translate some Eastern metaphors and principles when our cultural roots are different.

Some people in recovery may also develop psychic abilities and believe that this is the "powerful" end result. They may fixate on being psychic, which can end again in ego inflation. Our reward for working through ego inflation is *humility:* the solid foundation of an authentically spiritual, healthy and whole human being. With humility we are willing to continue learning throughout our lives. In this openness we are free not only to avoid any of the pitfalls of ego inflation, but we are also free to experience a connection with our Higher Self and Higher Power. In this state of humility and "second innocence," we can more easily and consciously experience whatever comes up for us.

Some experience ego inflation to a small extent and others may get stuck in it. The secret is to work on ourselves psychologically as well as spiritually. To believe we can be instantly healed is to attempt what we call a *spiritual bypass.* We try to bypass or ignore the lower to get to the higher levels of consciousness. Eventually, however, our false self will pull us back until we work through our particular unfinished business. Other names for spiritual bypass are *high-level denial* and *premature transcendence.* This is seen in any number of situations, from being prematurely "born again" to having a spiritual awakening and focusing only on the "Light," or focusing on psychic ability as a major part of our identity, to becoming attached to a guru or "path" in a detrimental fashion.

The consequences of a spiritual bypass are often active codependence or conflict: denial of the richness of our inner life; trying to control oneself or others; all-or-none thinking and behaving; feelings of fear, shame and confusion; high tolerance for inappropriate behavior; frustration, addiction, compulsion, relapse, and unnecessary pain and suffering.

If we live from our ego or false self, we feel separated and alienated, empty and with no meaning. We can only experientially connect with God, each other and ourselves by developing our True Self. Ego inflation and spiritual bypass are more cognitive or intellectual experiences, or "head trips." Being our True Self and connecting spiritually with God is more of a heart experience.

The way out of this trap is to harness the power of humility (that is, being open to learning more about self, others and God) and working through the pain of wherever we may be, or just enjoying being at peace when it happens. Those who are actively addicted, troubled or disordered can work through a Stage One full recovery program. Those who are also adult children of dysfunctional families can work through Stage Two recovery. We cannot let go of something if we don't know experientially what it is that we are letting go. We cannot transcend the unhealed. We usually cannot connect experientially to the God of our understanding until we know our True Self, our own heart.

If we can expand our beliefs and bring our higher nature into our everyday lives—we can experience true humility. Tuning in to God's unconditionally loving energy invites us to stretch beyond the limits of who we thought we were and become all that we are. This process allows us to experience a healing unity with ourselves, each other and God.

Basic to understanding the power of humility in resolving most conflicts with others is to know what triangles are and how they work, which we will now address in Part Two.

PART TWO

THE
UNCONSCIOUS
DANCE

Chapter 5

Level 1 Triangles

A triangle is an unhealthy relationship among three people. Whenever the pain of a two-person relationship becomes unbearable, one or both of them may bring in and involve a third person, place or thing to help relieve their pain. This forms a triangle, as shown in Figure 5.1. Healthy boundaries help prevent involvement in unhealthy triangles and their painful consequences.

Figure 5.1

Common Dynamics in the Formation of a Triangle

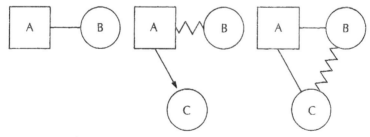

Source: From Kerr and Bowen, 1988.

The left diagram in Figure 5.1 shows a calm relationship in which neither person is sufficiently uncomfortable to triangle-in a third person, place or thing. The center illustrates the occurrence of conflict and unbearable pain. The more uncomfortable person, A, who also may be the less recovered or self-actualized, triangles a third person, C, into the conflict. The right diagram shows that as a result a substantial amount of conflict and pain has transferred mostly out of the original twosome and into the relationship between B and C.

An example: Mother, father and child are relatively calm. If mother and father have a conflict they cannot resolve, one of them may involve the child in such a way that their conflict and pain is transferred to an interaction between the other two. (Involving the child in this way may also occur with the participation of both parents, usually through unconscious collusion.) Similar to what happens in projective identification,[22] where one person avoids owning and dealing with their own inner life material, the formed triangle takes away the responsibility that the mother and father could take upon themselves to work through their conflict. This original conflict *did not belong to the child.* Yet by forming the triangle the parents are teaching their child unhealthy boundaries by modeling them. And they are wounding the child by forcing him or her to take on what is not the child's.

HISTORY 5.1: MARY'S STORY

Mary, a thirty-five-year-old stay-at-home mother with three young children saw me (CW) several times in individual therapy before asking her husband to join us. Her presenting complaints included low self-esteem, anxiety and an inability to get along with her children, especially the middle child who was a nine-year-old boy. They also had a daughter eleven and a son five.

Mary's husband refused to come at first and then agreed when we decided to make this a family session and invited the children. He arrived with their eleven-year-old daughter, and Mary came with their two sons. The daughter and father shared a two-seat sofa while the others took individual chairs. During the session conflict arose between Mary and the nine-year-old son. This held our attention through most of the session, and when I tried to move us on, the attention always came back to Mary and this one son. A few moments before the session was over, her husband stood up (and the daughter stood immediately upon seeing her father stand) and announced that none of this had anything to do with him, and the two of them walked out. Mary had several more sessions with me before realizing that her main conflict was with her husband, who had triangled her children into their numerous and painful differences. He chose not to engage her in working through their conflicts with or without triangling in one or more of their children. As an individual, Mary learned through individual and group therapy to de-triangle—she learned to take the conflict away from her children, allowing them to be children—and to look more closely at her strained relationship with her husband. Nine years later with the two older children away at college, she observed her husband triangling in their youngest child. Unable to stop the toxic triangle and feeling stronger, she divorced her husband. She now reports a healthier relationship with all three children and herself, including now having a higher self-esteem and lessening of her anxiety. In retrospect, she chose to let go of her need to be right and opened to trusting God, both of which are key characteristics of humility.

By contrast, in a healthy family, mother and father resolve their own conflict between themselves, even though they each may have to tolerate for a while the emotional pain that goes with it. By doing so, they model and teach their child healthy boundaries and, when appropriate, explain what may be happening should the child appear concerned.

The concept of triangles is old: "Three is a crowd." They exist in all families and in all human relationships. The only question is the number, intensity and composition of the triangles in one's life.

In recovery, which includes learning to set healthy boundaries, we can gradually discover how to identify and disengage from— and sometimes even avoid getting involved in—triangles. And the more recovered, self-actualized or differentiated each of the three people in an old triangle may become, the greater the chance that they may even be able to change it into a healthier threesome and move up to the Level 2 triangle, which we will discuss in later chapters.

A THREESOME

Let us begin to look at the characteristics of people who can begin to move away from conflict and up into the Level 2 triangle. A "threesome" is the interaction of three healthy two-way relationships (see Table 5.1). Each member functions from their True Self, and thus with authenticity and spontaneity. While it is an open system with flexible movement among the three people, there is closeness or even intimacy experienced between each of the three pairs. The awareness of their own inner lives (Figure 5.2) by each member generally tends to be high, and boundaries are generally healthy. In fact, it is the healthy boundaries that assist in keeping the threesome intact, in part because they help keep the twosomes intact.

Table 5.1 Triangle and Threesome: Some Differentiating Characteristics

Characteristic	Threesome	Triangle
Condition	Healthy	Unhealthy
Definition	Three healthy two-way relationships	An unhealthy three-way relationship
Awareness of Our Inner Life by Each Member	High awareness	Low to absent awareness
Consciousness of Each Member	Mostly True Self	Mostly false self
System	Open	Closed
Spontaneity	Mostly present	Usually absent
Movement	Flexible	Fixed, rigid or reciprocal
Interaction	Closeness	Fusion
Boundaries	Healthy	Unhealthy

Most triangles cannot be transformed into a threesome because it is unusual for each of the three members of the triangle to work through a process of recovery to a sufficient degree at around the same time. In this book, we will share ways of doing this. If only one or two of the three are willing to do this work, the frequency of triangular interactions and their detrimental consequences may decrease remarkably.

Figure 5.2 My Inner Life

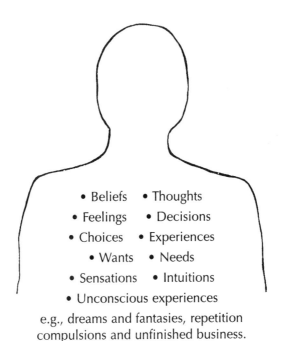

- Beliefs • Thoughts
- Feelings • Decisions
- Choices • Experiences
- Wants • Needs
- Sensations • Intuitions
- Unconscious experiences
e.g., dreams and fantasies, repetition compulsions and unfinished business.

TRIANGLES AND FUSION

A triangle is thus an unhealthy three-way relationship. Each member functions mostly from their false self, with little spontaneity. It tends to be a closed system with fixed, rigid or reciprocal movement. While there may superficially appear to be closeness among the members, there is actually usually only *fusion*, wherein one person overlaps another so that there is an indistinctness of self-identification or self-differentiation (see Figure 5.3). What overlaps are usually aspects of the two people's inner life and behavior. It is difficult to tell what is self and what is the other person, and it is difficult to tell where self ends and the other begins. We usually learn fusion (also called *enmeshment*) experientially in our family of origin.[23]

Figure 5.3 The Parents Enmesh the Children

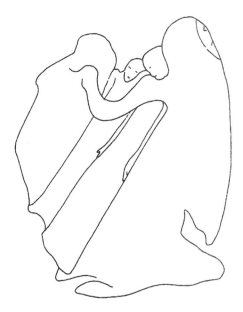

Source: Drawing from P. Morand, et al: *The art of Romaine Brooks,* 1967.

Seeking the impossible goal of completeness and fulfillment through another person, place or thing, any of the following can occur:

- One person may try to merge into the other, in an all-or-none fashion, to gain self-realization. (I am right and you are wrong, or you are right and I am wrong.)
- Two people may try to merge into one. (We always agree.)
- One person may lose themself in the other person. (I live for only you.)
- One person may usually pursue and the other usually distance, with little or no mutuality in their relationship.

When they get into conflict and the emotional tension gets too high for either to deal with, one or both of them may triangle-in a third person to lessen the tension. In a triangle the awareness of their own inner life by each member tends to be low to absent, and the unhealthy boundaries prevent the autonomy and individuation required to avoid the triangle, and they promote and maintain fusion. Each person doesn't have a realized True Self from which to be aware and to act appropriately, in part because they have no healthy boundaries to maintain the integrity of their True Self when it emerges.

THE ORIGIN OF TRIANGLES

The purpose of a triangle is to stabilize the two-person system when it is in danger of disintegrating. If two people can get interested in or distracted by a third person, object, issue or fantasy, they can avoid facing the real, threatening or scary issues between them. Ultimately, the triangle helps us avoid changing ourselves and our part of the problem. By contrast, two people sharing in common interest or activity in a healthy way or working through a conflict can nourish and enrich their relationship. Triangles are learned both inside and outside our family of origin. They are a product of how wounded and unrecovered or undifferentiated its members are. The more unrecovered the people are, the more important is the role of triangling for preserving emotional stability in a particular group of people. If there is relative calm, even in a family with very wounded and undifferentiated people, the three members of a triangle may function for a time as emotionally separate individuals. Because change and stress trigger fear and other painful feelings, an increase in these will tend to reactivate the dynamics of the triangle. In a well-differentiated system, such as a threesome, the members can maintain their emotional separateness and autonomy even when they are highly stressed. If people can maintain their emotional autonomy, functioning as their True Self with healthy boundaries, triangling is minimal, and the system's stability does not depend on it.

STABILITY

Triangles are not simple mechanical events, but are often complex interactions that have both personal (intrapsychic) and relationship (systemic) origins, dynamics, experiences and meanings. For example, the *stability* of any twosome can vary just by adding or taking away a third person, depending upon whether the relationship is stable or unstable at the time (see Table 5.2). These examples illustrate the many potential guises by which triangles may present themselves in stable and unstable relationships. Note, however, that here "stable" does not necessarily mean healthy, nor does "unstable" always mean unhealthy. Note also that a fused or enmeshed relationship may destabilize at any time, because it is not usually made up of two recovered or individuated people having a healthy relationship.

Table 5.2 The Stability of a Relationship May Vary by Adding or Removing a Third Person

If the Twosome Is:	It Can Be Destabilized By:	Example:
Stable	**Adding** a third person	Birth of a child in a harmonious marriage.
	Removing a third person	No longer able to triangle their child, parents fight more after child leaves home.
Unstable	**Adding** a third person	Birth of a child into a conflicted marriage.
	Removing a third person	Two people avoid a person who takes sides on issues in their relationship, which foments conflict by emotionally polarizing the couple.

Source: Compiled from Kerr and Bowen, 1988

SYMPTOMS AND CONSEQUENCES

Other ways that triangles may show their complexity are by their symptoms, which frequently are also their consequences. These may include:

1. *The original, unresolved conflict and pain* that wounds people and thus predisposes them to be involved in triangles. Without realizing and living from and as our True Self—with healthy boundaries to protect and maintain its integrity—it will be difficult to avoid being involved in triangles to such a degree. This woundedness usually comes from growing up in a dysfunctional family and society, where triangles are universal. Most people grow up learning triangles, not healthy twosomes and threesomes.

2. *A lost, hurting self* then results from that original wounding. This can be manifested by recurring illness in any one or more of the physical, mental, emotional[24] and spiritual realms[25] of our lives. Because our True Self is in hiding to survive, we come to rely upon our false self to run our lives. Not living from and as our True Self, we are left with the whims of our false self, which thrives on dysfunctional relationships, including regular involvement in triangles.

3. *Unhealthy boundaries* are both a basis for and a manifestation of being involved in triangles. Without boundaries and limits we cannot protect and maintain our True Self that keeps us in healthy relationships and out of unhealthy ones, including triangles.

4. *Inner and outer confusion, pain and chaos,* usually with some interim periods of numbness and sometimes calm. A reduction in the frequency and intensity of this chaos and pain, as well as improved functioning in relationships—all of which feels better—results from working through the long process of recovery.

5. *Repetition compulsions* may also be a symptom and consequence of being involved in triangles. In fact, regular involvement in triangles is itself a kind of repetition compulsion. Repetition compulsions are making the same mistake over and over.

6. *Scapegoating* is identifying one person, place or thing in the triangle as being the victim or the problem. Underneath we can see that all three members are at the same time victim, problem and potential solution. As family therapist Tom Fogarty describes, "Father and mother may avoid marital strife by focusing on their son. That is one part of a triangle. Son and mother avoid facing the difficulties in their over-closeness by having a common enemy—father. Father and son avoid dealing with their distance by relating to each other indirectly through mother. There is no victimizer or victim here. . . . All members of this triangle participate equally in perpetuating the triangle and no triangle can persist without the active cooperation of its members."[26]

However, given two wounded and dysfunctional parents, the young child cannot inherently protect itself against their damage and come out unscathed. By triangling in their child, the parents invade its boundaries and damage its True Self, thereby wounding the child. In later life the child, now adult, can heal his or her wounds by taking responsibility for his or her own recovery, in part by knowing these dynamics and then experientially working through and grieving the pain that they produced.

7. *Avoidance of closeness and intimacy* in relationships where these would be appropriate is both a cause and a result of triangles. We can use healthy boundaries to help avoid triangles, so we can focus on our wants and needs from our own inner life as we interact with our partners. Doing so promotes closeness and intimacy.

8. *Other symptoms and consequences,* including the creating of interlocking triangles, which we describe after Bobbi's story.

HISTORY 5.2: BOBBI'S STORY

Bobbi became the sixth member of our women's psychotherapy group that had been working together successfully for quite some time. This particular group was an example of empathy growing into unconditional love for one another and ourselves. After observing for two or three sessions, Bobbi shared with the group her inability to trust women. As a child she watched her mother and her mother's two sisters argue all the time. Her mother than "pitted" her and her brother against each other. She remembers always being in the middle when her parents were together—usually they ignored each other, only tending to Bobbi's needs. Now Bobbi says she can't hold a job for very long because she winds up getting involved in the office politics. Because she is the last one to be hired, when the tension in the office "blows up," she gets the blame, and feels like a victim.

Over time, we watched the group struggle with some negativity that Bobbi named and complained about first. The group couldn't identify it until one member finally brought up the gossip and laughter going on in the parking lot before and after group. When the group explored these loud and sometimes insulting moments, they reminisced about how unconditionally loving and empathetic the group had been until lately. Over time one member after another gently confronted Bobbi with something hostile she had said either outside group in the parking lot or inside before group had begun. There was no malice during these gentle confrontations. As a persecutor, Bobbi tried to blame the group, saying that she "could never get along with women," and this was a "perfect example of the persecution" she had endured. Her attitude was, "Either I'm right—or you're right. And I trust myself, but not you!" After several weeks of this, Bobbi slumped in her chair upon hearing the same comments from the group and said, "I'm doing what my mother did. I've had a good teacher." For a moment Bobbi let herself open to more possibilities than her controlling ego would have previously allowed. She worked on her need to control, which she said came from all the pain she absorbed in her childhood. She realized that learning more about herself (through humility) was her way out. We watched her take responsibility for some of the chaos in her life. And, as she struggled with her pain, she also explored more and more avenues for helping herself recover.

INTERLOCKING TRIANGLES

Interlocking triangles occur when the pain of one triangle, unable to be contained, overflows into one or more other triangles. In a calm family, one central triangle can for a while contain most of its emotional pain. But under stress, this pain spreads to other family triangles and to triangles outside the family in the person's work and society. This process is illustrated in Figure 5.4.

Figure 5.4 Example of a Family Triangle

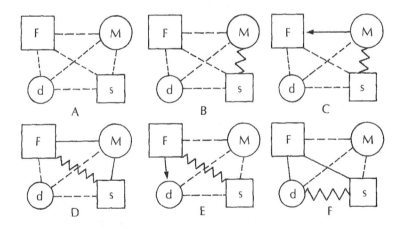

Diagram of a Family: with a father, mother, older daughter and younger son. A: all the triangles are fairly inactive. B: tension develops between mother and son. C: father becomes triangled into the tension between mother and son. D: tension shifts to the father and son relationship. E. mother withdraws and the original triangle becomes inactive. Meanwhile the daughter is triangled into the father-son tension. F: conflict erupts between the two siblings. So tension originally present in one triangle is acted out in another triangle.

Modified from Kerr and Bowen, 1988

MEMBER ROLES

The Pain "Generator"

In addition to the roles of scapegoat and victim already mentioned, members of a triangle often have rigid roles that create the triangle, maintain it and keep them locked into it. For example, some members may, by their behavior, tend to generate emotional pain in themselves and the others, and can be called pain *generators*. These generators, or *persecutors*, set the emotional tone of many of the members, may upset people and may be the first to get upset about potential problems, although they may not be the cause of that pain (see "Bobbi's Story").

The Pain "Amplifier" and "Dampener"

A second role is that of pain *amplifiers*, who add to the problem through their inability to stay calm and stay out of the conflict if it doesn't belong to them. A third role is that of the *dampeners* who use emotional distance to control their reactivity to the others' behaviors. Under higher stress, people in this role become overly responsible for others in order to calm things down. While dampeners may on the surface reduce some of the symptoms and consequences, they reinforce the creation and maintenance of the triangle. We can also call this role the *rescuer.*

Abuser, Enabler and Other Roles

Other roles may also influence the dynamics of the triangle. These include the role of the *abuser,* which, like the pain generator, or persecutor, is one of the most intimidating and dysfunctional roles. Another is the *enabler,* who unconsciously—and sometimes consciously—facilitates the destructive behavior of a dysfunctional person. This facilitating may include repeated attempts to rescue or fix the dysfunctional person. Still other roles are those described by authors and clinicians Sharon Wegscheider-Cruse and Claudia Black: the family *hero* (responsible or successful one), the *lost child* (the adjuster or quiet one), and the family *mascot* or *pet* (little princess, Daddy's little girl or Momma's boy). Each of these roles may add their own dysfunctional aspects to the rigid and stereotypical behavior of any member of a triangle.

Guises of Unhealthy Dependence

Because most people who are regularly involved in triangles tend to fit the description of being actively co-dependent, a member of a triangle may also play any of the roles that we described as guises of unhealthy dependence. In addition to some of the roles mentioned, these guises may include: people-pleaser, overachiever, inadequate one or failure, perfectionist, victim, martyr, addicted, compulsive, grandiose and selfish or narcissistic one.

HISTORY 5.3: DONNA'S STORY

Donna checked in every week at her psychotherapy group with short reports on a conflict she was having with a close girlfriend of hers. Finally, she asked for time to work on the growing pain she was feeling. Her friend Sally had a new boyfriend who seemed to be a model date. Sally had repeated "bad luck" with boyfriends who always wound up emotionally and psychologically abusing her. This man talked to her during the week with e-mails, and then they saw each other on weekends. Sally forwarded every e-mail to Donna to get her opinion of what he was writing that was wrong. When Donna told the group about this, they validated her opinion that the boyfriend wasn't saying anything wrong in the e-mails and sounded like a nice man. Donna went back to Sally and told her that her friend was not doing anything to hurt her and that her emotional upheaval over his letters was unfounded. Donna reported at the next group that Sally then turned on her and told Donna in an angry and attacking tone that *she* was part of the problem. Donna worked on her past pain with women, especially her mother and several girlfriends who frequently triangled her into other conflicts they were having. She realized that she had taken on the tension that belonged with the other two people. Instead of Sally dealing directly with her conflict with her new boyfriend, she had transferred that painful conflict (from her past) onto Donna. Sally was seeing her new boyfriend free of tension because she had found a third person who would take it.

Donna told Sally she needed a few weeks to sort out what had happened between them. Doing so gave her more time to process her feelings, wants and needs regarding their conflict by setting a healthy boundary. Then she sat down with Sally with the hope of talking it all out. Donna told the group, "I realized an hour into the superficial banter that there was no way Sally could or would talk about it. So I have removed myself from this triangle by removing myself from the degree of investment that I previously had in the friendship."

Each of the various roles, guises and traits can bring different aspects to the behavior of a member of a triangle. In recovery, a person may draw upon any of these less desirable traits as they transform them into healthier ones. For example, martyrs or victims can learn to be more sensitive to their inner life and take responsibility for making their life a success, which would include learning to set healthy boundaries. An example from Donna's story is the boundary she set first by putting time and space between them and then by not pitying or feeling sorry for Sally, which would have kept both of them in conflict.

⁃⊗⊗⊗⁃

With any three people, one triangle is possible. Add but one more person, and now there are four potential triangles. Add another for a total of five people, and there are ten. By all of the above examples and dynamics in this chapter, we can begin to see how common, pervasive, contagious and destructive triangles may be. Is there a way out?

Chapter 6

How to Get Out of Unhealthy Triangles

Unhealthy triangles (which we call Level 1 triangles) are common, and avoiding and getting out of them is not easy. To avoid them we can take several actions, including attaining a *healthy self,* which includes being an *autonomous, individuated* or *self-actualized* person, all of which can lead to and benefit from having healthy boundaries.

We can keep on the lookout for involvement in triangles by having an *awareness* of them when they are occurring or are about to occur. We can also learn and *develop skills* to detriangle, including being real, being creative, and having emotional autonomy. Finally, we can institute all of the above by taking *action* to avoid or get out of the triangle, which we will explain below.

While we have discussed the common and traditional view of triangles and how to get out of them, in this book we also offer a potentially new perspective. That perspective brings us from a victimized and polarized posture with life (Level 1 triangle) to an empowered and co-committed relationship with life (Level 2 triangle). As we begin to realize that our reality is a result of our choices, we empower our True Self and take on a co-creative stance with life (Level 3 triangle) that ultimately leads us to actualizing our true nature (Level 4 triangle). In this model, we move from an external view as mirrored by others to an internal point of reference of ourselves, allowing a nonjudgmental view of where we are now. We accept where we are without blame or guilt for our life situation. From a position of unconditional acceptance of our life's walk, we can nurture a relationship with life that witnesses its events as opportunities to grow rather than as crises that imprison us. Finally, as was shown in the map of the mind in Chapter 4, (see page 39) we can realize our relationship with our True Self, Higher Self and Higher Power as Sacred Person.

Throughout all of this process is the underlying practice of *taking responsibility* for getting into an unhealthy triangle in the first place and for getting out of it, as well as for owning all of our own inner-life material as it comes up for us in each of the two relationships of the triangle.

In the previous chapter, we said that triangles are not simple mechanical events. Rather, they are often complex interactions that have personal (intrapsychic, inner life) and relationship (systemic) origins, dynamics, experiences and meanings. In this chapter, we will describe several important relationship issues in triangles. But in the sparse literature that is available on triangles, there has been little written on their personal and intrapsychic aspects, which we will now describe.

USING PERSONAL MATERIAL TO DE-TRIANGLE

Personal material, such as repetition compulsions and abreactions, may distract us from de-triangling. Repetitions and repetition compulsions are when we make the same mistake over and over or continue the same behavior that is detrimental to self or others. They tend to be behavioral and experiential reenactments of our original traumas, as shown in Figure 6.1.

Another example of personal material may include abreactions and flashbacks, which are generally a more dramatic form of age regression. Age regression happens when we suddenly feel upset, confused and scared like a helpless little child. There may be no apparent cause for it, and it may last a few minutes or longer. One minute we are an adult feeling okay, and in a matter of seconds we feel like an out-of-control and helpless child. Abreactions and flashbacks are a kind of reenacting and reexperiencing of past traumas from a perspective of our total being—including our physical, mental, emotional and spiritual aspects.[27]

These are important to remember as we reach for the higher levels of triangles, because our "unfinished business" will pull us back down to unnecessary pain and suffering if we are not conscious. Unfinished business may interfere with having a healthy self and healthy relationship. Exploring, owning and working through what is ours, that is, healing our unfinished business, can enhance having a healthy self. These principles are also useful to get out of a triangle, whether it is an old or new one.

Figure 6.1 Examples of Dynamics in Repetitions and Repetition Compulsions

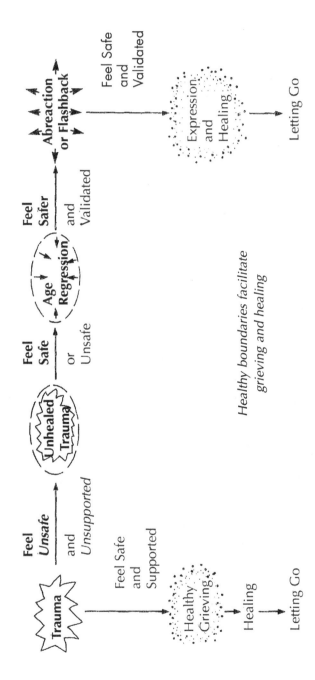

Figure 6.2 My Inner Triangle

M = myself; C = person with whom I am in conflict; WH = my wished-for helper

From this perspective we can illustrate the members of a triangle as being *myself* (shown as M in Figure 6.2), the person with whom I am in *conflict* (C) and the *wished-for helper* (WH), the third member whom I may unconsciously triangle in to help relieve the tension that I feel from the conflict.

Once I am involved in such a triangle, I can help myself by exploring what each of these three may represent for me within my own deepest self. In doing so, I may discover that as part of the triangle, inside "me" (M) is a *conflict of dualities*. Each of the other two members of the triangle represents one of the two opposites in that particular duality (see Table 6.1). For example, the person with whom I am in conflict (C) may remind me of my *"bad" parent* who prevents me from getting what I want or need. My wished-for helper (WH) may remind me of my *"good" parent* who helps me get what I want or need.

Table 6.1 Personal or Intrapsychic Roles

Member of Triangle:	Myself (M)
Intrapsychic Representation	Conflict dualities within my psyche, whether conscious or unconscious.
Projection	I project aspects or parts of my unhealed inner life onto the two others.
Repetition Compulsion	I keep setting up triangles . . .
Awareness & Work Before Recovery	I am usually aware of most of this conflict.
Wanting Help	I have to discover or remember that I am the one to work through my conflicts.
Awareness & Work During Recovery	My job is to work through the conflicts in my *inner* triangle.
Feeling Safe	I search for safety in my inner life.
Related Core Issues (Examples)	**Feelings** Fear of **abandonment** Need to **control** **All-or-none** (dualities) **High tolerance** for inappropriate behavior
Detriangling	• Be real and objective • Work through my feelings • Set healthy boundaries • Can get help from a safe and skilled person outside the triangle
After Recovery	I have healed most of my conflict.
Healthy Threesome	I work on myself, set healthy boundaries and include God.

and Dynamics in Members of Triangles

Person with Whom I am in Conflict (C)	Wished-for-Helper (WH)
May remind me of my "bad" parent, etc.	May remind me of my "good" parent, etc.
I project the more painful onto aspects of my unhealed inner life onto this person.	I project the less painful aspects this person.
. . . in order to work through my conflict that this person represents	. . . or that this one represents, or both of them.
This person may not be recovering/recovered and aware.	Neither may this person.
I would like something from this person, though I am not getting it.	I ask this person for help, directly or indirectly.
Provides the conflict.	May or may not help me to resolve the conflict. May make the conflict worse.
I feel less safe with this person.	I feel safer with this person right now.
They may have same or similar core issues.	They may have same or similar core issues, plus being over-responsible.
As during recovery (above) or after recovery (below).	As during recovery (above) or after recovery (below).
I will set healthy boundaries with this kind of person in the future.	I (or we) will select only safe people and keep healthy boundaries, asking them more specifically what I want from them (e.g., just listen, give feedback, etc.).
I avoid closeness with toxic people.	Same as under (M) and (C).

In other words, I go inside myself and into my past—through my present conflict—to tease out any parts of my having been wounded. I can do this by using any of a number of experiential techniques, such as telling my story to safe people, writing in my journal or working through conflicts (also called transferences) in my individual or group therapy.[28]

As I work through my being stuck in a particular triangle, I can consider several other aspects of my inner life to help me de-triangle. These may include:

- My projections (what parts of my unfinished business I may have projected onto the two others)
- Repetition compulsions (Do I keep setting up these kinds of triangles?)
- My awareness of being in a triangle
- My work to de-triangle
- The responsibility that we take to work through all of this conflict

I can also consider how safe I may feel going into my inner life. At first, I may be so unfamiliar with certain aspects of my inner life, such as feelings, wants and needs, that it feels uncomfortable to go into it. And it is always uncomfortable to stay with or tolerate the emotional pain during any conflict. So a major part of recovery is learning to *tolerate emotional pain* while I work through my conflicts as they may come up in my day-to-day life.

When I *make the connection* between my present conflict and my past unhealed conflict in both an *experiential* and a *cognitive* way, I am then free to *grieve* and thereby release the stored painful energy from my original unhealed trauma. Doing so can assist me in eventually releasing myself from the triangle.

USING BOUNDARIES

A major aid in de-triangling is setting healthy boundaries and limits. When I am in a conflict with another person, I set my boundaries so that I do not triangle in a third person. If the person with whom I am in conflict tries to bring in a third person, I can likewise stay detached from becoming involved with them by maintaining my boundaries. Crucial to all of this is having a healthy and autonomous self, which means that I am as fully aware as possible of and live from my True Self. (This is one way to work with the conflicts. We will introduce other ways in future chapters—ways that include perceptions of connectedness and unity.) It is because I have a healthy self that I can set healthy boundaries. This then frees me to focus on working through the conflict that I have with the other person.

If I find myself triangling into the conflicts of two others, I can likewise set my boundaries. If I do not have a healthy sense of myself, or self-esteem, I may feel the need to try to fill my own emptiness by getting closer to them through joining in their conflict. But it is at just this time that I can maintain emotional autonomy by working instead through my own issues, such as perhaps feeling like an outsider. Family therapists Michael Kerr and

Murray Bowen said, "Three people, together for a brief period of time, will invariably gravitate to a process of two insiders and one outsider. Well-differentiated (recovered, self-actualized) people do not make a 'federal case' out of being an outsider, nor does their emotional security depend on being one of the insiders."[29]

USING ROLES AND DYNAMICS TO DE-TRIANGLE

Using the roles of *persecutor, victim* and *rescuer,* Stephen Karpman has described the following dynamics in triangles.[30] (See also sidebar below, "The Karpman Drama Triangle.") Being vigilant for these dynamics may help us avoid triangles or get out of them:

1. A triangle tends to start with my not being real and honest.
    a. If I am dishonest with someone, whether it is about information, my feelings or experience, I may immediately enter a triangle.
    b. "Shoulds" will also pull me into a triangle. Perceiving or being told that we should do this, should behave like that or should feel this way encourages us toward expressions that we don't naturally feel. Perhaps *the* most important part of healing is learning how to go about getting my needs and wants met after learning to distinguish them from my "shoulds"—the things that other people have *told* me are my needs.
2. It hurts to be in an unhealthy triangle. All positions in such a triangle are painful.

3. There is no personal power in Level 1 triangles. No matter what role I am playing, I am operating from a lack of honesty and a loss of personal power.

4. Most people have a favorite starting role or position, usually rescuer or victim. Few initially choose to be a persecutor, unless perhaps as a defensive, preemptive tactic.

5. Once involved in a triangle, most people end up playing *all three* positions. For example, I may have perceived myself as a rescuer who wound up as someone's victim, while at the same time that person perceives me as being their persecutor.

6. Guilt and other painful feelings tend to hook me into a triangle.

   a. When I feel guilty, it is a signal that someone is attempting to pull me into a triangle.

   b. To stay out of a triangle, I can give myself permission to feel guilty without acting on it. In other words, I do not let the guilt push me into any of the roles.

   c. Thus, I learn to be uncomfortable and sit with the guilt.

   d. Other painful feelings, such as fear, shame and anger, may likewise hook me into a triangle. I can work through these also.

7. The "escape hatch" out of a triangle is often located in the persecutor position. Being real, telling the truth and expressing my feelings opens the escape hatch out of the triangle. To stay out of, or to leave, the triangle, I have to be willing for the other two to perceive me as the bad person.

This does not mean that I am the bad guy, but the others may choose to see me that way. If I am not willing to be seen as a persecutor, I will likely get hooked into rescuing and put myself back in the triangle's tension.

In the process of leaving the triangle, I am beginning to be more aware of my inner life, including my feelings, wants and needs, plus my motives around being in the triangle. Open to being my True Self with healthy boundaries, I am willing to experience my feelings and to let others experience their feelings without having to rescue them. If the other people in the triangle are willing to experience their feelings and to tell their truth, the triangle will likely dissolve. If they are not, as is more common, then I may leave looking like the bad guy.

8. I can also play out a triangle alone. Raised in a dysfunctional family, I may not need another person to push me into a triangle.

    a. Playing a triangle alone happens when I listen to the negative voices inside my head that beat me up, put me down and constantly *shoulds* me. These old tapes usually come from a dysfunctional family and society. This *should-er* is my false self.

    b. Remember, shoulds are untrue. They have nothing to do with who I am, who others are or how healthy relationships work. They are someone else's interpretation of what to do and what is "good" or "bad."

    c. When I play a triangle with myself, my *should-er* will

persecute me so that I will feel like a victim. At the same time I will be feeling guilt, fear, shame and/or anger. These feelings may trigger the belief that I am a persecutor and drive me to rescue someone (or some situation), even when listening to my old tapes is what is trying to manipulate me into the rescuer position.

9. When I actively participate in a relationship with someone who lives in a triangle, I can be *vigilant for hooks*. It is difficult to be around people who constantly operate in triangles and not get hooked into them, especially if my personal boundaries are not clear and I have not learned to recognize triangles.

10. My internalized *should-er* is also the voice that pushes me into a triangle when the other two members are attempting to hook me. As my false self, the *should-er* is the part inside me that stores my old tapes, but that I may mistakenly believe is my True Self. It is negative, rigid, controlling, perfectionistic and self-righteous. Unattached to this false self, I would likely not participate in a triangle.

12. Being in a triangle is not being fully alive. It is a kind of living death. It is a life of inauthenticity, pain and lack of acceptance and love.

12. *Being real*—telling the truth and experiencing my feelings, with healthy boundaries—is a way out of the triangle. I have to learn to know and define my boundaries and take responsibility for recognizing, experiencing, expressing and completing what comes up in my inner life appropriately

with safe people—and sometimes with unsafe people. We can consider and explore whether we can apply some of these principles to experiencing being in others' roles in triangles.

The Karpman Drama Triangle: In Review

Many professional counselors, psychologists, clergy, physicians and workers in the field of addiction are aware of a drama triangle that clarifies the victim position. The concept originated with Stephen Karpman in his work studying domestic violence.[31] From his studies, he originally described the dynamics of the triangular relationship between wife, husband, and the police.

Karpman, working within the school of *transactional analysis,* has identified an interactional pattern he calls the "drama triangle." The three points of the triangle are called *victim, persecutor* and *rescuer.* An example of this kind of triangle encountered frequently by police and therapists is the domestic dispute. A battering spouse may enact the persecutor role, and the partner the role of victim. If the police, or therapist, assumes the role of being the victim's rescuer, it frequently happens that the roles all shift: The victim persecutes the rescuer (the police) who in turn is rescued by the original persecutor who now tries to quiet down the original victim. The "remainder" or "fallout" from the conflictual interaction of any two players gets passed around the triangle like a hot potato, all three players "catching it" on a rotation basis whenever it becomes their turn to play rescuer. This game, which could well develop into a game without end, corresponds to what Murray Bowen refers to when he says that triangles are often more stable than dyads.

The drama triangle describes how many of our conflicts in three-way relationships are handled. Have you ever had two roommates, business partners or perhaps two siblings sharing your intimate space? In such a relationship of three, there is often two against one in any given decision. If the two-against-one dynamic doesn't seem to rotate frequently, soon the losing member begins to feel isolated, ganged up on, *victimized* and feels a loss of control and power in the relationship.

This may also occur outside of domestic disputes and three-way relationships. In fact, these patterns and conflicts may also exist *inside* each of us as we described on page 73. Since Jung first described his archetypes within the collective unconscious, we have known that we incorporate psychological patterns of relating to each other and ourselves. The transactional analysis model that illuminated Karpman's drama triangle used adult, child, and parent as important primary inner and dynamic roles. (Magenson 1976)[32]

THE RELATIONSHIPS

I do not have to discontinue my relationships with people or divorce myself from them in order to de-triangle. Indeed, if I choose, I can still relate to either or both of them in a healthy way. Relating in a healthy way involves establishing a relationship with each person separately, with each relationship having its own integrity and unique character, rather than developing an *alliance* with either person *against* the other. But by having a healthy self with healthy boundaries, I am better able to sort out just what is mine and what is not mine, and not get involved in or take on their conflicts. The ability to be in emotional contact with others, yet remain autonomous in one's own emotional functioning, is the essence of the concept of differentiation.[33]

We can get involved in triangles with members of our families, friends, acquaintances, bosses or supervisors, colleagues and peers, teachers, spouses, lovers or others. Perhaps the most common situation is where I am already in a relationship with two others and a conflict develops between two of us. At that time either of us may triangle the third into our conflict, or the third may enter spontaneously. The third may also not be a person, but could be a pet, idea, ideology, cause, place, thing, behavior, group or another object.

WATCHING FOR OTHER DYNAMICS

There are four additional dynamics that may occur in a Level 1 triangle: a *power difference, role reversal,* being in a *double bind* and *secrets.* Each or a combination of these may either draw us into a triangle or make us feel stuck in one. Knowing about them may prevent both.

Power Difference

In a power difference, one or two of the members have some kind of power over the other member or members that can be destructive to each individual and to their relationships as three people. For example, two parents have power over their child, who is vulnerable to their behaviors and whims. With this difference in power, unless the parents are themselves healthy or recovered, there is little likelihood that they can have three healthy two-way relationships. Or a boss has two employees, and when they become triangled, her power as boss may clearly influence their relationships and the triangle. Of course, the child and the employees may have their own forms of power, which may set up still more variations within the triangles.

As we recover, we learn that there are different kinds of power. Moving from its most primitive to its most effective and sophisticated, at the lower end is power as *physical strength,* which can also include financial influence. Next is power as *manipulation* (maneuvering to get things indirectly), followed by *persuasion* and then *assertion.* These may all be used by parents and the boss above, and to some extent even by the child and the employees. These are the lowest levels of power.

But depending on the circumstances, there are more effective kinds of power, including *watchful waiting* (the *wu-wei* of Taoism), *accepting* and then *letting go.* When I truly let go of something that is toxic or not mine anyway, I no longer beat myself up about it, thus freeing myself to experience a more successful and enjoyable life. Continuing to the top of the spectrum of power, the next most powerful is *wisdom,* then *compassion,* and finally the most powerful is *unconditional love.*

Each of these various kinds of power, from the most obvious and primitive to the most sophisticated and effective, may be used at different times to get out of a triangle once in one, and to avoid getting into one if doing so can be anticipated. In employing each of these, we claim and use our personal power. We reclaim our personal power through a process of increasing awareness and by taking responsibility for our well-being and functioning:

Power = Awareness + Responsibility

Part of that power is activated by setting healthy boundaries and limits.

HISTORY 6.1: SUSAN'S STORY

Susan is in Stage Two recovery. She lost her best friend, Toni, in a sudden accident when she was twenty-nine. Susan and her husband remained close to Toni's husband, Jack, during the first few years of mourning. With the now-widower Jack able to date again and form a relationship with a woman, he stopped seeing Susan and only occasionally saw her husband. Susan came to me (BW) with an overwhelming sense of disappointment and anger. "Losing my best friend was out of my control—losing Jack is terrible. He hasn't died! We were close before and went through all that pain together, and now he just walks away from us as though we don't matter. I don't even know this girl. I only met her twice, and yet I am in this painful triangle with her and Jack. I have built up a resentment against her because she has taken Jack away from us. I resent both of them now because it feels as though Jack has abandoned us. While I have some abandonment issues that go back to my parents and ex-husband's emotional abandonment of me, this doesn't feel like that. Rather, I feel like this whole thing is out of control. I can sit back and wait without feeding any energy into this. But every so often the feelings boil up, and I feel like I'm going to explode. I think the most painful part is I have no control over what has happened."

When we worked on her concerns about feeling stuck in this Level 1 triangle, she said she felt like the victim of both Jack and his girlfriend. She was able to connect this back to her ex-husband and parents' never connecting with her emotionally. By working on and through her current and past conflicts, Susan realized that her ex-husband's affairs with other women had hurt her so deeply that she was now transferring some of that conflict and pain onto her relationship with Jack. She realized that the occasional rage that boiled up was a transference of her conflict and pain when her ex-husband ignored her and gave his girlfriends the attention that she felt she deserved. With this insight regarding both her external *and internal* triangles, and through prayer, she was able to move herself to a Level 2 triangle (which we discuss in Chapter 7), from feeling like a victim to a more empowered person and self.

Role Reversal

In a role reversal one person in a relationship takes on parts of another's role that should not belong to them. The child attends to Daddy's needs over the long term, when the reverse should occur. Unable to have a healthy intimate relationship with him, his wife may collude with the child. The child becomes the caretaker to the parent, as the parent places his needs above the child's. Yet the parent does not give up control. In his narcissistic and manipulative way, he also often plays the child off against his mate. Even though the child is unable to be a child, she feels chosen and special, at times a variation on "Daddy's little girl," and tries always to be "good." Which of these set up and maintained the original triangle? Daddy's narcissism? Mother's distance? Both parents' trauma effects? Probably all of these did.

As the girl grows up, some of the destructive consequences of the triangle become more pronounced in her life. She becomes "depressed" when she is unable to care for her father, does not know her True Self, is over-responsible for others in many of her relationships and cannot function in a healthy twosome or threesome. To get free of such a triangle involves a long and winding process, which we describe in Stage Two recovery in Chapter 7. A crucial part of this healing will include naming what happened to us (some of which may be: mistreatment [abuse or neglect], triangulation, role reversal and lost selfhood) and then experientially realizing our True Self, which results in healthy boundaries.

Double Binds

In a double bind there is no safe or healthy place for us to go. We are damned if we do and damned if we don't. The child in the above family triangle is in a double bind. If she continues to give to her father while sacrificing herself, she will lose her selfhood. But if she speaks up for her needs, her narcissistic father, for whom she can never do or be enough, will shame her, and her mother will likely guilt her. She is caught and cannot leave. As an adult, her discovering, naming accurately and knowing this information and these dynamics can help in her total recovery.

Double binds often originate in a family or other setting where the child cannot leave the setting and has neither the cognitive or emotional capabilities to formulate a solution. Growing into adulthood, the child may continue to perceive—and through repetition compulsions or re-enactments to recreate—situations in which there are usually no safe alternatives for resolution.

Double binds are common in triangles, and they always contain an implied threat. Persons caught in one usually abandon themselves by inappropriately letting down their own boundaries and compromising their needs. Because most people who become regularly and strongly involved in triangles are not yet recovered enough to be able to recognize that they are in them or how to get out, being stuck in this kind of situation is hard to deal with. Asking for help from a safe, skilled therapist can be a start.

Secrets

Another dynamic in Level 1 triangles is having one or more secrets. One or two of the members may have a secret, which may influence the triangle in some way. It could even be used as a point of "power" at times. But secrets are usually destructive to the individuals and their relationships.

Toxic Secrets: A secret is anything we are *told not to tell*, or anything important that people may keep from one another. There are two kinds of secrets: healthy and toxic. Keeping a *toxic secret* can be damaging to us and to others. It may lower our self-esteem, increase our guilt, block our ability to grieve our losses and hurts (which may be part of the secret), and weaken our immune system. In short, it may block our peace and serenity.

Healthy Secrets: A *healthy secret* is a confidence. It is private. If we keep a healthy secret, we and others will not be harmed.

Holding something in such a sacred way can aid healing. It respects its keeper(s).

We do not have to go out now and tell all of our secrets or even someone else's secret. What tends to be more healing and helpful for us in de-triangling is that (1) we come to know any important secrets that may have been kept from us, and (2) we tell to a safe person any toxic secret that may be harming us—or that may harm them if they do not know the secret.[34]

Toxic Secrets can produce Level 1 triangles. Usually occurring in a boundary violation, critical knowledge or behavior (the secret) is kept from another. This withholding of important information gives the secret-holder an unfair advantage in the relationship. A person with a secret can take on the illusion of having "power" over the other two. If he tells one of them (the colluder) the secret and not the third member (the outsider), he has set up a Level 1 triangle. In a boundary violation, secrets may either (1) separate one or two of the members of a triangle while deceitfully maintaining the pretense of a common interest or endeavor, or (2) superficially join the two who know the secret against the outsider.

Keeping the secret is toxic to all three members of the triangle because it destroys trust, conceals information that the other(s) may need to know and erodes the relationships. Because the keeper(s) of the secret so often act out of *the secret*, rather than from their True Self, they may withhold an important part of communication, closeness or intimacy in their relationships. Sometimes the real secret is not about the content of the information but rather about the motive or intent of the keeper(s) of the secret. All of these dynamics tend to stabilize and maintain the triangles.

For obvious reasons and because of their nature, secrets are among the most difficult for the unknowing person to deal with in any relationship, whether with only one person or more people. To help in de-triangling it is helpful for the unknowing person who suddenly discovers an important secret to work through the shock and pain in a constructive and healing way. Part of this healing will likely include sharing the secret and feelings about it with safe people. These safe people may include a best friend, a therapist or counselor, a therapy group, or a self-help fellowship group.

For the *knowing* person(s), secrets are also difficult to deal with, though in a different way. Should they decide to help themselves de-triangle by telling the secret, they will likely have to handle their resulting feelings of guilt, shame and fear, in addition to lost trust from the previously unknowing person. Deciding to tell and then telling is a delicate balance. It may also *harm* the unknowing person or others, as the Ninth Step of the Twelve Steps addresses: "Made direct amends to such people wherever possible, except when to do so would harm them or others." (The Eighth Step reads: "Made a list of all persons we have harmed, and became willing to make amends to them all.") Not knowing a secret can be more harmful (and thus toxic) than knowing it, even when it may be painful to tell it and to know it. But should secret-keepers decide not to tell their secrets, they may have to live with those painful feelings long term, in addition to always having to remember and watch what they say to the unknowing person.

In Level 1 triangles, one or more of these dynamics is often present. They may interact, and they may aggravate and maintain the triangle. And when the present triangle is unable to contain all of the pain of each of its members, it may spread to and interlock with one or more other triangles.

USING SPIRITUALITY

So far we have focused on two basic relationships: with *self* and with *others*. But there is a third relationship that we can use, if we so choose, and that is with the God of our understanding. After we have done everything that we know to do to avoid or get out of a triangle, we can also ask our Higher Power for assistance.

These two actions—doing what I can do and then letting God do the rest—are the components of the process of co-creation. While I can ask for this assistance and turn over whatever it may be that I need help with at any time in the process, it is most helpful if I have also first done *all that I can do*. I can ask and turn over all this remaining pain through prayer, meditation or any other way that I commune with God.

—∞∞—

These two chapters (5 and 6) form a strong base for understanding the dynamics in our day-to-day and ongoing conflicts. Whenever we are in pain or find ourself projecting it onto another, it may be useful to review them.

While it may offer some relief to the tension between the original two people in conflict, staying in a Level 1 triangle also distracts the two from working through it, in addition to all of the painful effects described in the previous chapter. With the assistance of the knowledge and skills contained in this book and elsewhere, we can strengthen our ability to have healthier relationships and to avoid becoming involved in unhealthy triangles.

In the next chapters we offer a way out of the unnecessary pain and suffering that we self-inflict in the all-too-common triangles in which we find ourselves.

PART THREE

THE POWER
OF HUMILITY

First, one understands that he causes much of his own
suffering needlessly.
Second, he looks for the reasons for this in his own life.
To look is to have confidence in one's own ability to end
the suffering.
Finally, a wish arises to find a path to peace,
For all beings desire happiness.
All wish to find their purest selves.

—The young Dalai Lama in the film *Kundun*, 1997

Chapter 7

Level 2 Triangles: From Conflict to Co-commitment

When we find ourselves in the painful conflict of a Level 1 triangle, whether in our relationships or internally—in our inner life—we may have more choices than we think. In addition to the ways to de-triangle described in the previous chapter, we can also consider some other ways out.

Being caught in the conflict of a triangle appears to offer us two choices. The first is to stop participating in the triangle, as we described in Chapter 6. The second is not to get involved in a triangle in the first place. However, there may be special circumstances in some triangles wherein we can consider more expanded and productive ways to handle such conflicts. In this chapter we will explain some of these other choices for de-triangling by using methods and skills that offer us more flexibility. This expanded way of viewing conflicted relationships and triangles is a major focus of this book.

Level 1 triangles tend to be more rigid and cause emotional and sometimes physical pain for each of its members. They tend to be ego driven, fearful, and based on shame, guilt and anger. They often operate out of the two most common core recovery issues of adult children of trauma in early recovery: *all-or-none* thinking and behaving, and needing to be in *control.*

By contrast, Level 2 triangles offer us more flexibility. In place of *victim, rescuer* and *persecutor,* the roles now become expanded into *self-empowered, nurturer,* and *motivator.* This new triangle tends to be True Self driven and in the long run has less resultant suffering. This is because in Level 1 triangles we usually resist pain—which creates our suffering. In Level 2 we know we have pain, but allow for it, which then creates awareness, opportunity and movement of our pain.

Instead of feeling conflicted, stuck, frustrated and powerless, Level 2 thinking, behaving, and being is based on seeing more choices, feeling empathy and realizing acceptance through conflict, all of which are based on co-commitment instead of conflict.

RETAINING LEVEL 1
DE-TRIANGLING ADVANTAGES

A basic principle when moving from one triangle to a higher level is that while each progressively higher level *transcends* one or more levels below it, it also includes and subsumes those below. For example, when moving from a Level 1 triangle to a Level 2, we do not have to discard perhaps the most useful relationship skills, which we use in the healthy practice of de-triangling, *of choosing not to participate* in a triangle at all.

Instead, we can relate to each of the triangle's other two members in a healthy and relatively conflict-free way, while at the same time transcending into a Level 2 triangle.

SOME QUESTIONS AND POSSIBLE ANSWERS

Our "attitude" toward living describes our relationship with life. Do we embrace life or resist it? Do we consider having a curiosity about how our life works? Or do we have a need to control people, places and things to stay at a distance? Do we allow our life to unfold? Is our life a friend or a foe? As we explore these questions, we may cultivate an attitude that opens our awareness to considering the empowerment that we derive from an expanded Level 2 triangle. To develop such a positive attitude we can begin by letting go of some of our limiting ego-driven traits, including those of judging, blaming and guilting others.

LETTING GO OF JUDGMENT, BLAME AND GUILT

How do we let go of living in all-or-none, right-or-wrong, or either-or thinking? Can we give up feelings of powerlessness, helpless-hopeless and choicelessness? Can we be mindful of releasing the right to judge another person's perception of reality—believing that there is only *one* version of reality (that is, ours)?

Can we let go of feeling we are victims? Can we choose to accept our responsibilities, i.e., accept ownership for all of our perceptions of reality and the meaning that we give them?

REFRAMING

When we de-triangle, we can see what happens to our prior Level 1 triangle roles of victim, rescuer and persecutor. We shift from feeling like a victim to a position of empowerment. In doing so, we use the skill of *reframing* the conflict that was formerly "victimizing" us.

Reframing implies looking at something from a different perspective. Our view gets bigger, more inclusive and encompassing. The reframe, the expanded perception(s) contain more information, cognitively and emotionally. Our prior victim stance no longer holds the power it had over us. We learn to see the dark and the light, the yin and the yang, as parts of the process. We see the wholeness and balance in things. We embrace any oppositional energy as a challenge. Or we let it go.

We sometimes see the positives that unfold after seemingly terrible life events. Divorce, job loss, serious accidents and illness usually bring us to a victim stance. When we open to the challenge that comes with these painful conflicts and experiences, our grieving can help us identify with our True Self, expanding our thoughts and vision. Collectively, economic, social and political disasters can bring people together and unite a nation, as we saw during the first year after September 11, 2001. But living in our false self can aggravate such unity, as we saw in the subsequent political conflict aggravated by our all-or-none two-party political system (see side bar, "Raising Politics to Level 2").

Raising Politics to Level 2

The past two presidential elections (2000 and 2004) have been painful to watch and are examples of some of the dynamics we find in Level 1 triangles. In these two elections both political parties in their conflict had visions of being rescued by the voters. Each claimed to be abused by the other party. Each took turns being victim and abuser. We were often tugged back and forth and then triangled-in even more by our friends and family who were voting differently than we were. The triangles continued after the election: separation, polarity, accusations and, unfortunately, little movement—only toxic frustration.

Trauma psychologist Robert Geffner, Ph.D., wrote: "It appears that the United States is now a more polarized country than in the 1960s, when we were in the midst of civil rights issues, or in the 1970s, when Vietnam was of major concern. The outcome of the U.S. elections and the various exit polls and comments is further support of the polarization. The United States media continue to focus and talk about "red" states and "blue" ones as if somehow that is all that matters."[35]

A solution: Raise our awareness and behavior to the second level of co-commitment after the election by each polarized party calling for a unified government and nation. We as a nation can motivate ourselves to end our differences and unite for four years so we can get things done. This takes humility and courage by embracing a new way of being. When will our politicians lead us with integrity? Of course, a driving force for this polarity is the ego-oriented, all-or-none two-party system. Perhaps now is the time for us to hold our politicians responsible for not acting with integrity and instead, making the good of the nation and the world come first.

HUMILITY AND THE TWELVE STEPS

A substantial number of people in recovery have used a Twelve Step fellowship recovery program. It takes humility to begin to work the Twelve Steps of recovery from any life problem. To admit we are powerless over anything, and that our lives have become unmanageable, is difficult. To even consider these possibilities takes an opening within our inner life. Hitting a "bottom" is often a factor. A small degree of humility may allow for that beginning. Then, when we start to work the Twelve Steps, that degree of humility begins to grow—usually slowly. The more humility we have, the more we can work the Steps. And in a reciprocal fashion, the more we work the Steps, the more our humility grows, as shown in Figure 7.1. The more both of these increase, the more we recover and heal. (See Appendix B for further examples from Steps Six and Seven.)

Figure 7.1 Humility, Working the Twelve Steps and Healing
A Reciprocal Relationship

EXPANDING LEVEL 1 ROLES

When we expand our view of a Level 1 triangle, each role can change to allow and promote inner peace. We now transform our persecutor role into that of a *motivator* (see Table 7.1). As a motivator we no longer judge or blame the victim. We often can stop projecting our own painful feelings onto the victim. We become a sort of cheerleader. We have an interior attitude that communicates affirmation: "I know you can do it! It may be a tough choice, but I believe in you."

Table 7.1 Roles in Level 1 and 2 Triangles

Level 1	Level 2
Victim	Empowered Self
Persecutor	Motivator
Rescuer	Nurturer

These expanded roles offer us still more choices. The person formerly in the rescuer role in the first triangle, having dropped the internal victim, and now believing in the choice-making potential of the former "victim," transforms this position into a *nurturing* role. A nurturer emotionally supports the person faced with a difficult situation, problem or choice. And the former "victim" takes responsibility for remaining in a victim stance and reframes their attitude and behavior into a more *empowered* person (see Table 7.1 and Figure 7.2).

Figure 7.2 Roles in Levels 1 and 2 Triangles

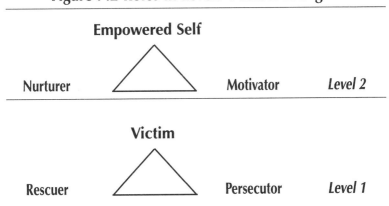

Thus we see the emergence of a higher functioning Level 2 triangle, which we can also call a *co-commitment* triangle, a term first suggested by Gay and Kathryn Hendricks in their book *Conscious Loving: The Journey to Co-Commitment:*

> A co-committed relationship is one in which two or more people support each other in being whole, complete individuals. The commitment is to going all the way, to letting the relationship be the catalyst for the individuals to express their full potential and creativity. In a co-committed relationship between two people, each take 100 percent responsibility for his or her life and for the results that each creates. There are no victims in co-committed relationships. In fact, victimhood is impossible when both people are willing to acknowledge that they are the cause of what happens to them. There is little conflict, because neither person plays the accusatory, victim role. With the energy saved through lessened conflict, both people are free to express more creativity.[36]

HISTORY 7.1: LAURA'S STORY

Laura was thirty-eight years old and a member of our psychotherapy group for two and a half years. She came from a moderately dysfunctional family and childhood—as did her husband. As she worked on her issues over that time she realized that her twelve-year-old son, Jason, was enmeshed in a triangle with her and her husband. She realized that her feeling of being their victim came from both her son and husband, but was really more about her dysfunctional marriage that she couldn't change. She saw herself as constantly placating to her husband and as a victim between him and their child. Over time she understood her role in this Level 1 triangle and brought her husband in for several couples therapy sessions with me (CW). He was not interested in therapy. He remained passive or said he wanted to leave. During a couples workshop that she had insisted they take, he told her that he wanted to end the marriage; he was sick of the conflicts and felt she had never been on his side. Laura said she realized at that point that he would never understand how important her personal growth and recovery was. She agreed to divorce. They both agreed for Jason's sake they would drop their resentments toward each other and continue to co-parent, only now they would be on the same team for the good of their child. They started reframing their conflicts to include what was good for Jason and for their mutual peace. Over time, Jason's behavior improved and so did his grades in school. Laura is encouraged by this and continues to work on her recovery.

Both Laura and her husband feel more empowered and less likely to blame the other. For now, they have transcended Level 1 triangle functioning and are living a more evolved and successful Level 2. When the pressure was off their child, he was able to return to being a child.

At this level of functioning, it becomes necessary to be able to identify clearly our needs for nourishment and nurturing, expressing them without repression or the need to manipulate others unconsciously in order to get our needs met. Laura's story is an example of giving up the stance of all-or-none, either/or polarity and agreeing to be on the same side, which gives room for expanded both/and successful resolution.

CO-COMMITMENT

The first triangle—briefly described as conflict—operates through negative thinking and relating. It is based on competition for a falsely perceived scarcity of nurturing and love. The second triangle—*co-commitment*—is based on cooperation, positive thoughts and relationship patterns of support, respect and responsibility for one's choices. As shown in Table 7.2, this Level 2 triangle has transformed scarcity to abundance, from "not enough love" (attention, power, money) to "I have the power to nurture myself and the clarity to ask for love or attention when I need it"—an empowered quality or position.

The Level 2 triangle thus becomes a relationship dynamic

marked by co-commitment with others. Here the "commitment" refers to having and maintaining an inner integrity to our own authenticity, awareness and willingness to respect all perceptions, preferences and needs. Our choices come from an empowerment within. It is *not* located outside of us. We are no longer focusing outside of ourselves.

To move to Level 2 we open our hearts. Therefore, it is in and around the heart chakra where most of our work takes place. The challenge is one of attaining balance. The abundance of Level 2 begins to bring *more* to our lives: It offers us more possibilities, choices, decisions and experiences. For some, the realization that it is possible to assume responsibility for all our reality can feel overwhelming. Others may just glance at it and retreat into denial and a feeling of numbness. In spite of the difficulties in attaining it, being in Level 2 is noticeably peaceful and more enjoyable.

We learn to live in our hearts (instead of our painful "codependent" feelings that come from focusing outside of ourselves). As we move up the triangles, each new step both includes and transcends the previous triangle(s). As we benefit from our new peace in Level 2, we accept more dimensions of our life, identify our wounds, become more aware of our painful patterns, reframe our way of thinking, open our hearts and increase our choices.

Table 7.2 Characteristics of Levels 1 and Level 2 Triangles

Areas of Attention	Level One Conflict (ego)	Level Two Co-commitment (True Self)
Stance or Story	Victim or martyr	Telling our story; authentic
Parenting	Controlling; shaming	Supportive; empowering
Roles/Polarities/ Energies	Victim; rescuer; persecutor	Self-empowered; nurturer; motivator
Primary Characteristics	Fear based: choiceless, powerless; emotionally supports choicelessness; right and wrong thinking	Acceptance through conflict; can see choices; can be empathetic win-win
Chakra	Root—first through third	Heart—fourth
Triangle Maintenance	Competition for nurturing or nourishment; fear of change, failure; avoid fear; staying in control	Active and aware; expressing and listening
Triangle Initiation/ Embracing the Shadow	Relieve tension of dyad; simple presence of third person; playing the game	Tired of suffering; crave/seek a better way; self-knowledge and expression; expose authentic expression; give up the games
Transformation of Suffering	Being "pushed by suffering"	Pain, not suffering

Areas of Attention	Level One Conflict (ego)	Level Two Co-commitment (True Self)
Power, Act, How You Meet It	Embrace the contrary, duality and opposites	Accept; balance
Energy That Drives It	Desperation, survival drive (feminine); toxic frustration (masculine)	Courage; leap of faith; longing for peace, unity and a better way
Spiritual Practices	Conventional religion	Meditation, prayer, yoga, Twelve Step work; psychotherapy (humanistic, existential, transpersonal); Stage Two Recovery (such as trauma-based); body/breath work; indigenous practices
Hindrances	Awareness, recovery	Conventional religion, psychology, medicine, politics, business, media; mind control/ ego; fear; doubt; shadow; intellectualization of life
Humility	Absent; arrogance (often hiding shame) and denial	Begins true expression

In the sidebar below, we offer some guidelines for being in these higher levels.

**Guidelines for a Grounded and
More Peaceful Inner Life in the Higher Levels**

1. No manipulating (exerting shrewd or devious influence, especially for one's own advantage).

2. No projection of our "stuff" (assigning or "dumping" our issues, pain or unfinished business) onto others.

3. No denial or invalidation of others' reality (such as their feelings, preferences and other aspects of their inner life).

4. Stay as conscious as possible.

5. No need to "win." Being "right" could be the booby prize.

6. Strive to support significant others.

We will likely find it useful to practice being in and even enjoying Level 2 triangles before rushing into Level 3. While at times we may find prayer useful to move up to Level 3, there may be no rush for us to try to jump there prematurely.

Chapter 8

Level 3 Triangles: From Co-commitment to Co-creation

If people can look
Into each other's eyes
With love
And truth in their hearts
Anything is possible.

—*Barbara Whitfield*

Moving into Level 3 being and functioning is usually made easier by accomplishing several tasks. These include (1) having completed substantial *recovery work* in Stages One and Two (as described on pages 43 and 112), (2) engaging in daily *spiritual practice* long term, and (3) having developed a significant and consistent degree of *humility*.

STAGES ONE AND TWO HEALING

Stabilizing and healing any active Stage One disorder or illness are basic to being able to heal, over time, from the effects of trauma. We described this process briefly in Chapter 4 (page 42), and have discussed it in more detail in *My Recovery: A Personal Plan for Healing.* Unless these two large and crucial tasks are accomplished, it is usually difficult, if not impossible, to move consistently into Level 3 being and relating. Looking back at the map of the mind in Chapter 4, without substantial healing in Stages One and Two work, we will likely continue to live from our false self. Completing this work allows us to live from and as our True Self most of the time. It is our True Self that experientially knows self, others and God. If we haven't completed our work, our false self will lead us to believe that we are in Level 3 when in fact we are spinning our thoughts into a head trip that may inflate our ego/false self.

HISTORY 8.1: SUSAN'S STORY CONTINUED

Susan (introduced in Chapter 6) recently heard that Jack, the old friend who had ignored her, was marrying the woman he had dated for a few years. Susan and her husband were not invited to the wedding—only family was invited. Susan explained in group therapy, "I started doing my old "them against me;" I'm right and they're wrong. This woman is just like all the other women in my life who hurt me. I watched a cascade of hurts wash over me. Then I remembered I have choices now. So I invited in my Higher Self to help. Instead of the duality of them against me—I suddenly felt compassion for myself, which felt a lot better than the anger museum I had carried. I realized how sad my history is when it comes to women, starting with my mother, and the compassion turned into my inner parent soothing and taking care of me. Jack's on his own journey now. I need to take care of myself!"

Susan added that practicing meditation and praying each day, although hard in the beginning, helped her to bridge her connection to a Power greater than herself.

DAILY SPIRITUAL PRACTICE

Daily meditation, prayer, spiritual readings or the like are important. Doing these greases the wheels of our personal and spiritual awareness, and maintains and nourishes us as we strengthen our humility.

When I move from the Level 1 triangle to Level 2, I observe myself in my relationship to God. I can see clearly how I relate to myself and others. I move from a more constricted, limited view to one of exploration and possibility. I begin to see my life as a moving and dynamic process. We open ourselves by surrendering our preconceived ideas of how things are and allow ourselves *not to know*.

Cultivating the strength to "not know" allows others to be themselves around us. It allows for different interpretations of the same event. It allows us to reframe our own point of view. We learn to balance our life in the vision that pulls us toward our True Self and into the teaching of the Level 3 triangle. Life becomes our meditation practice and our Higher Self becomes visible in our daily activity. We'll discuss this practice further in Chapter 9.

HUMILITY

Having and using our increasing humility is a key to moving to higher functioning. Without it personal growth is usually impossible. Our humility will help us to work in an easier way with our feelings. Instead of telling ourselves stories about why we feel a particular way, we can accept the ability to be still with our feelings and let them move through us. A sense of movement and/or a bittersweet tone will accompany our holding painful feelings. Stories at Level 3 get in the way of feeling. A large part of recovery is about learning to tolerate and hold painful feelings while we work through them and finally let them go. Feeling our painful emotions allows us to move through them with compassion for self and others. From the first moment we attempt to leave a Level 1 triangle we will benefit from taking with us the skill to tolerate emotional pain. This skill is a major part of the foundation for recovery and for developing our humility.[37]

EXPANDED ROLES

In Level 1, the roles in the triangle were *persecutor, victim,* and *rescuer.* In Level 2 these expanded to *motivator, empowered self,* and *nurturer.* All of these have characteristics of being nouns, roles, and they reflect polarity. But the language of the Level 3 triangle takes on a more dynamic quality, often using action-oriented words. In Level 3 these roles-in-action become creativity, energy/movement/vibration, and love and expansion, as we show in Table 8.1 and Figure 8.1.

Table 8.1 Roles in Levels 1, 2 and 3 Triangles

Level 1	Level 2	Level 3
Victim	Empowered self	Creativity
Persecutor	Motivator	Energy, movement, vibration
Rescuer	Nurturer	Love and expansion

Figure 8.1 Visual of Roles in Levels 1, 2 and 3 Triangles

Creativity

3

Co-creation

Love and Expansion   **Energy, Movement, Vibration**

Empowered Self

2

Co-commitment

Nurturer   **Motivator**

Victim

1

Conflict

Rescuer   **Persecutor**

PRIMARY CHARACTERISTICS

The primary characteristics of Level 1 thinking and being are fear based, all-or-none and thus limited. Expanding to Level 2, our primary characteristics are choice making, empathy and realizing acceptance through conflict. In Level 3, Co-creation, we live from and as our True Self now expanded to our Higher Self. Our primary characteristics at this level are expanded to vision, compassion for self and others, and Co-creation with God. We can begin to clarify Level 3 functioning with the following history.

HISTORY 8.2: ED AND MARSHA'S STORY

Ed's daughter Bonnie moved from the eastern seaboard to Colorado. She saw her father and stepmother, Marsha, yearly when she went east to visit.

At age thirty Bonnie called and told them her live-in relationship had ended and she had just found out she was pregnant. Ed and Marsha invited her to come and live with them while she had the baby, and they would then help her raise it. Bonnie returned, and together they celebrated the birth of the child, a boy named Christopher.

Marsha and Ed provided day care while Bonnie worked to support herself and her baby. On Chris's first birthday, Bonnie told Marsha and Ed that she was saving her money to return to Colorado. For the next year and a half they were in a triangle— Bonnie, Marsha and Ed, and Colorado (places or things can sometimes be part of a triangle). When Bonnie talked about moving, Marsha and Ed retreated into themselves and found comfort only in prayer.

Finally the day came when the moving van left and Bonnie and Chris kissed Ed and Marsha good-bye. Everyone cried. For the next several weeks Marsha and Ed actively grieved. They felt their hearts had been torn apart and at this painful time all they could do was pray. They prayed for their child and grandchild's safety and eventual happiness, for help in the pain they were cycling through, and for God's will. Their pain and their prayers took them deeper into humility. They realized they would go through it all over again—even the painful separation—because they knew they had helped give their grandson a good start. Now they had to have faith in Bonnie and faith in their relationship with God.

In Colorado, Bonnie met Drew who has a son, Paul, a year older than Chris. They fell in love and married. Bonnie and Chris are now living in the Rocky Mountains with Drew and they have had two more children.

Recently Ed and Marsha received an e-mail from Bonnie that ended with this paragraph:

Last night I showed Drew the slide show I made when I left Atlanta. He loved it. Lots of memories came back. I'm so happy we all got to share in Chris's birth. How did you know to invite me? My life will always be special because of it. So, looking back, I see it as an experience where I was given a choice, then chose the right path, all the while determined to return to my heart's home with my new child. During this time I was able to develop and strengthen my relationship with my father (and stepmom). I learned to balance wise choices with determination. Then I returned to my home and learned how to do it alone. Having been taught that it was okay to ask for help, I learned how to find this help in Boulder and anywhere else I looked."

Marsha and Ed stayed in Level 3 through prayer and letting go of their Level 1 need to control Bonnie by trying to keep the two of them from moving. Through their pain of letting her go they prayed and co-created love and expansion for their child. It turned out to be a win-win situation for everybody.

RELATIONSHIP WITH HIGHER POWER

When we enter and experience living in Level 2, we also open the door to a third level, accessing what some spiritual teachers have called "the third eye" chakra—a higher perception of life and a more soulful relationship with ourselves. In the story above, Marsha and Ed found a closer relationship with each other and God, in addition to a closer relationship with Bonnie and Chris. They moved into Level 3 through prayer, awareness, grieving and letting go. This moved them into a new way of being that they couldn't have predicted. It opened them even more to using the attitude and skill of humility.

To move into the third level, we need to develop our relationship with a higher part of ourselves, our Higher Self, as we show in the map of the mind in Chapter 4 (page 39). We also experience a nurturing relationship with God. Our relationship to our

Higher Power changes as we develop and grow, both personally and collectively. We are no longer alone in our abilities to be creative. Now, we lovingly ask for help in our action of co-creation. We also see the Mystery beginning to reveal itself in what we have come to call synchronicities. Meaningful coincidences, synchronicities happen all the time, although we may not notice them among the otherwise ordinary occurrences in our day-to-day lives. Level 3 brings us to a new conscious awareness that shows us more of these synchronicities and gives us an appreciation that our lives are being woven from a higher meaning. Some have called them "cosmic postcards."

At this level there is *one part of our attention always on God*— focused on the "We" instead of the "I." Because of this aspect of "Divine Attention" we call it the *Co-creative Level.* We are co-creating with our Higher Power. We recognize this partnership. We experience a continuous flow of energy that helps us to create a life of peace and plenty.

Here the roles of the triangle again change. The *motivator* role of the second triangle become qualities of *movement, energy, vibration.* It is important to remember that the roles, as they evolve upward, move from nouns to action-oriented words; from roles toward qualities—divine qualities (see Table 8.2). These are the energies of the masculine: dynamic, action oriented and capable of manifestation. This newfound energy and action includes the *power* inherent in our inspirations, the force of a vision, of being *driven* by a creative project. The proverbial muse moves us— literally!

The *nurturer* role of the second triangle continues toward an alignment with *love* and *expansion*. This new feeling is an *emotional holding*, a deep compassion, and an ability to give and receive unconditional love—a divine feminine quality. This is the capacity to love those whose beliefs are contrary to ours. To love those that disagree with our most personally held perspectives. And to validate and embrace differences as divine.

The *empowered self* of the second triangle is now transformed into a co-creative energy and action. To be *co-creative* with God implies that we rejoice in the opportunities that conflicts hold for our now inspired choice making. Therefore, instead of avoiding conflicts, we learn to embrace and relish them as creative outlets. At this level of development, it is as if God and we become partners. We sense the flow and perfection of God in our life, we act in ways that creatively manifest our now expanded intent, and we love unconditionally while we do it. Dualism, right/wrong thinking and polarities no longer dominate our experience and reality. Some have called this state of being "Enlightenment," which we discuss in the next sidebar.

Table 8.2 Level 3 Triangle—
The Action/Energy of Co-creation

Level 2 Triangle (Nouns, Roles)	Level 3 Triangle (Oriented Toward Action)
Empowered Self	Creativity
Motivator	Energy, movement, vibration
Nurturer	Love and expansion; emotional holding

After Enlightenment, What Next?

We believe that the following excerpt from spiritual teacher and author Jennifer Hoffman helps clarify some of what we are saying in this section of this book. She uses the term "enlightenment" the way we use the higher levels of functioning.

There is a belief that the Shift in Consciousness *[moving up the Levels we describe]* will eventually mean the end of human existence as we know it. And that is partially true. Following that belief, though, is the hope that we will no longer have to experience life's trials and difficulties, that we will live lives free of drama and grief. And that is also partially true. But we will still be humans living in a human environment, and although we may achieve enlightenment, the learning is far from over.

There is a Taoist saying, "Before enlightenment, carry water. After enlightenment, carry water." We still have to make our way through the world, live our lives and navigate through the obstacles that appear on our path. Enlightenment does not entitle us to a life that is free of lessons or problems, all it does is make them easier to resolve, if we recognize the situations that we encounter and use the tools that we have acquired to resolve them. Enlightenment is empowering, and empowerment allows us to be in balance with the Universe. Now the next part of our spiritual journey can begin.

Our spiritual journey is not linear in nature, as we have believed from our third dimensional perspective [Level 1 thinking and functioning]. Rather, it is an evolutionary spiral whose core consists of our life lessons. Each time we are able to achieve enlightenment at a particular level, we move up along the spiral, facing our lessons from a different perspective. [See figure 8.2].

. . . The purpose of our life here is to grow spiritually. We do this by experiencing as many lessons as we can in order to gather enough spiritual tools to move us along our spiritual path. If we learn nothing from our lessons then we have not accomplished our objective because we are not here simply to experience lessons, but to learn from them. Each new lesson has its special gifts and blessings and one of our tasks is to find those gifts and blessings and to learn to appreciate them by learning from them. . . .

Source: Excerpted with permission from an article of the same name from the online magazine Planetlightworker.com by Jennifer Hoffman. © Jennifer Hoffman, 2005.

Our spiritual journey is an evolutionary spiral, as shown in Figure 8.2. Each loop of the spiral represents a lesson or growth cycle. And each lesson will usually be followed by another one and designed by us and our Higher Power to move us farther along our spiritual journey.

Figure 8.2 Recovery and Growth Through Experiencing, Telling Our Story and Observing It All
(from Whitfield 1987)

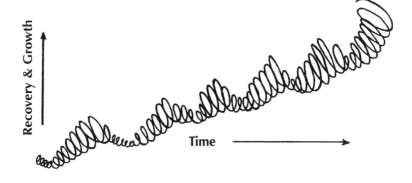

In the next chapter we address what we believe is the most unknown and difficult Level of the Four to experience. Yet, attaining it may be the ultimate goal of many spiritual seekers.

Chapter 9

Level 4 Triangles

As Rodgers and Hammerstein wrote in their musical *Oklahoma,* "Everything's up to date in Kansas City. They've gone about as far as they can go." While our life on this small planet and our relationship to God remain part of a Divine Mystery, we believe that reaching Level 4 being and functioning is about as far as we can go. Even so, only a few of us have experienced it.

We can begin to describe Level 4 as the ultimate peace and joy that we experience when we embody the essence of the Trilogy of God. The Trilogy includes God, God's unconditional loving energy for us (the Holy Spirit), and God's child, the Christ.[38] If the modern holy book *A Course in Miracles* is right that we humans have forgotten that each of us is also a Christ, then it is possible that at some time in our evolution, *we also* can experience Level 4 being. For most of us that peace and joy comes in brief glimpses. Contemplatives search for it. Many people use alcohol or drugs in search of it. Others use the Hollywood notion of "romance" to look for it. Many pray for it. By contrast, some say that it is our natural state, when we remove our ego and fear from its frequent distractions.

People in recovery from addictions have called part of it *serenity*, Eastern religions have called it *samadhi* or *sat-chit-ananda* (being-consciousness-bliss), *A Course in Miracles* calls it *Atonement* (pronounced At-*one*-ment), Richard Bucke called part of it *cosmic consciousness*, and others call it *Christ Consciousness*.

HISTORY 9.1: GREG'S STORY

This is an interview that one of us (BW) did in 2003 with Greg, then age sixteen. While at a church-sponsored work camp with his friends (they had just finished a new roof for an Appalachian house that was much in need of repair), Greg's close friend Kyle became acutely ill. He was helped to the nurse's office, disoriented and confused, by the nurse and one of the chaperoning fathers.

BW: Tell me what happened in your own words.

G: When I got in there, Kyle was lying down. The nurse's room was really small. We were all crowded in there, the nurse, Michelle's dad, and Kyle lying down on a cot. He was in his work clothes, with a bandana on his head that was mine, covered with a sleeping bag and still shaking really bad. I got in there and took one of his hands; the other was under the covers. Eventually I was holding both his hands. I didn't know anything about his condition, but they wanted him to drink some kind of Gatorade and he wouldn't.

I sort of knew he was in shock. He didn't really know what was going on. I tried to tell him not to worry and tried to give him some drink, but he gagged.

I got him to look right in my eyes. I said to him, "Breathe with me, Kyle." Then he started breathing normally. I didn't really know what happened or how this happened. I could tell that everything was coming back to him. I could tell he knew now what was going on.

BW: Later in the day, Kyle said that Christ was in you, and you had helped him to heal. How do you feel about that?

G: Well, I . . . I didn't feel like . . . I didn't feel like Christ. It felt good that I could help. I wasn't looking for recognition or for praise for what happened. It wasn't like that. I'm just glad I was able to help Kyle.

BW: Yes. I understand, and I hear humility.

G: Yeah. I definitely felt humbled. I felt something moving through me, like light or something. I cried the whole time. It felt like something was going through me to get to Kyle. It was incredible. I told him afterward that only three people will ever know what happened in that room—him, me and the Lord.

BW: But it sounds like the other kids felt it because there was a lot of crying going on when you told everyone else the story. Your friend, Frankie, said something like sixty-five kids were raised up by it. So could we say this was "contagious"?

G: Yeah. There was a brother and sister there who were fighting a lot, and all of a sudden they were seeing eye to eye. Everyone was getting along.

BW: I've done hands on healings and then written on how Spirit uses us as instruments. I found over the years that it never makes us arrogant, but it makes us humble. We have a direct relationship; it's a direct knowing instead of just believing that this is possible. We know it is possible because we can feel it coming through us. Can you comment on that?

G: Yeah. I definitely felt it, and then after it was like a breath of fresh air, kind of . . . a release. And I knew it, but I knew I didn't do it.

BW: Could we say, "We're conduits"? We're like empty tubes and it's coming through us?

G: Exactly!

BW: But we have to be willing. It only happens if we are willing. Do you think that somewhere in you there was that "click" of being willing—there was that moment?

G: Yeah! I have this thing with our Father. Every night when I go to bed I tell God about my day, and I thank him for it all. I am so grateful for every day.

BW: Have you always had this relationship with God?

G: No. It's been about two years.

BW: What do you think it is that happened two years ago?

G: I think I reached just a complete understanding and full appreciation for the Lord and everything he has provided me and that he provides me every day. An example of this would be my family. They are a miracle.

BW: Tell me about your family—that two years ago you realized they were a miracle.

G: Well, I always knew how important they were to me, but it's like once you begin having this powerful relationship with God, everything in your life takes on a new value. I always loved them, but I'm also so grateful.

BW: What do your parents do to help you? Is there anything special that they do?

G: They're hopeful and caring. They show a lot of love for each other and me. I see a really healthy relationship between them. I think it's a lot of things. I know for a fact that when I get married, I would want my relationship to be similar to theirs.

BW: Is there anything else you'd like to tell me about your spiritual life? Who you are spiritually?

G: I am truly grateful for everything in my life, for God; I trace everything back to him. He is the source of all the great things in my life. I pray every night, which I feel is a big part of why I have such a strong relationship with God. By praying every night or just whenever I want to—God seems closer to me and my heart and Heaven just doesn't seem like a destination above, but rather a place in my own heart. I personally thank God for everything in my life and for everything I have when I wake up every morning and when I go to bed every night.

BW: What do you think you're going to do in the future? Are you going to use this in any way?

G: Yeah. I probably want to be a teacher or a school counselor or a sports trainer. I'd love to be a part of a career that helps others. I understand how religion in public schools isn't generally accepted, but I would use everything I have learned, and I guess you could say this "gift" that I have, by applying it to everyday life.

I feel everyone possess this "gift" within them. The definition of the gift is simply just making others happy with something as simple as a smile. God's love isn't something hard to find. It's within everyone.

BW: If you could say anything else . . .

G: God is always with us. People tend to feel alone at times, but if they just opened the eyes of their hearts they would realize that he is always there. People can find God in themselves and in others.
. . . If people stop focusing on the negative aspects of others and themselves, God's love becomes present—making for a happier view of ourselves and of the world we live in.

Greg's experience gives us an example of Level 4 being and functioning. Grounded in this reality, it illustrates many of the characteristics of humility (as described in Chapter 2). Never owning this spontaneous healing as coming from himself, he attributes this remarkable moment to his and others' relationship with God. He continues this way of being in the way he sees God in others, especially in his parents' relationship with each other and their children. He goes on to look forward to a life where he will serve others. He uses prayer not to ask for things but to continue his ongoing relationship with a personal God that he knows in his heart.

READER/CUSTOMER CARE SURVEY

We care about your opinions! Please take a moment to fill out our online Reader Survey at **http://survey.hcibooks.com**.
As a **"THANK YOU"** you will receive a **VALUABLE INSTANT COUPON** towards future book purchases as well as a **SPECIAL GIFT** available only online! Or, you may mail this card back to us and we will send you a copy of our exciting catalog with your valuable coupon inside.

(PLEASE PRINT IN ALL CAPS)

First Name		MI.		Last Name	

Address					

State		Zip		Email		City

1. Gender
- ❑ Female
- ❑ Male

2. Age
- ❑ 8 or younger
- ❑ 9-12
- ❑ 13-16
- ❑ 17-20
- ❑ 21-30
- ❑ 31+

3. Did you receive this book as a gift?
- ❑ Yes
- ❑ No

4. Annual Household Income
- ❑ under $25,000
- ❑ $25,000 - $34,999
- ❑ $35,000 - $49,999
- ❑ $50,000 - $74,999
- ❑ over $75,000

5. What are the ages of the children living in your house?
- ❑ 0 - 14
- ❑ 15+

6. Marital Status
- ❑ Single
- ❑ Married
- ❑ Divorced
- ❑ Widowed

7. How did you find out about the book?
(please choose one)
- ❑ Recommendation
- ❑ Store Display
- ❑ Online
- ❑ Catalog/Mailing
- ❑ Interview/Review

8. Where do you usually buy books?
(please choose one)
- ❑ Bookstore
- ❑ Online
- ❑ Book Club/Mail Order
- ❑ Price Club (Sam's Club, Costco's, etc.)
- ❑ Retail Store (Target, Wal-Mart, etc.)

9. What subject do you enjoy reading about the most?
(please choose one)
- ❑ Parenting/Family
- ❑ Relationships
- ❑ Recovery/Addictions
- ❑ Health/Nutrition
- ❑ Christianity
- ❑ Spirituality/Inspiration
- ❑ Business Self-help
- ❑ Women's Issues
- ❑ Sports

10. What attracts you most to a book?
(please choose one)
- ❑ Title
- ❑ Cover Design
- ❑ Author
- ❑ Content

TAPE IN MIDDLE: DO NOT STAPLE

BUSINESS REPLY MAIL

FIRST-CLASS MAIL PERMIT NO 45 DEERFIELD BEACH, FL

POSTAGE WILL BE PAID BY ADDRESSEE

Health Communications, Inc.
3201 SW 15th Street
Deerfield Beach FL 33442-9875

FOLD HERE

Comments

SACRED GROUND

There is a dilemma when we try to talk about human relationships at Level 4. We are standing on new ground—or trying to climb to higher ground. Our map of the mind includes the Sacred Person: True Self, Higher Self and Higher Power as One. When we are totally alive and no longer need to spend any energy from our false self—our Sacred Person is the fourth level.

Our highest functioning friends tell us that when they ask for help as this threesome, almost immediately help comes in ways they could not have predicted. This help is softer and more loving than they could have imagined and comes with integrity and tenderness—there are no painful confrontations except an occasional loving confrontation where they are flooded with knowledge about themselves, the other person or the relationship. In such instances it appears they are in a meditative state or a life review.[39] And now, in this reality they feel what the other is feeling. They see the bigger picture. The reality of the other side is this reality, too. And they trust God's Divine Energy (Holy Spirit) to work in others as it is working in them. Table 9.1 shows us how Level 3 compares with the expanded spiritual awareness of Level 4.

Table 9.1 Characteristics of Level 3 and Level 4 Triangles

Areas of Attention	Level 3 Co-Creative, Higher Self	Level 4 Higher Power, Home, Unity Consciousness
Stance or Story	Mythic	Divine Play
Parenting	Accepting/allowing	Full Collaboration; Divinely creative
Roles/Polarities/ Energies	Creativity/love; expansion/energy; movement	Creator/God/Goddess/ All-That-Is/Christ Consciousness/Holy Spirit; "Om" vibration; Ruach Ha Kodesh
Primary Characteristics	Vision; compassion; creativity and expansion	Unity Consciousness; fully authentic and aware; harmony and vibratory bliss
Chakra	"Third Eye"— fifth and sixth	Crown—seventh
Triangle Maintenance	Relating to energy— not form	Merged with the Beloved (archetype)
Triangle Initiation/ Embracing the Shadow	Humility and aloneness; stepping out of the game	All-one-ness
Transformation of Suffering	"Letting go"; compassion; divine intelligence	Unconditional love; pulled by your vision
Power, Act, How You Meet It	Internalized Divine Authority	Vehicle of the Mystery
Energy That Drives It	Grace; stillness	Love in action; service; compassion
Spiritual Practices	Continued and deeper meditation; prayer; selfless service	Living life as the Presence of God
Hindrances	Ego; fear of losing self	Pressure of the collective unconscious
Humility	Builds; expressed	"Is" (fully expressed)

HISTORY 9.2 BARBARA'S LIFE REVIEW IN HER NEAR-DEATH EXPERIENCE

My life review during my near-death experience taught me what I now believe to be a Level 4 understanding. Others in my life were one in concert with me and God. Here I had no ego or fear—nothing to stop me from taking in what I needed to know. Humility was not an issue, because it seemed natural to me then.

God's love was holding me. It felt incredible. There are no words in the English language, or maybe in this reality, to explain the kind of love God emanates. God was *completely accepting* of everything we, God and I, reviewed in my life. . . .

In every scene of the review I could feel again what I had felt at various times in my life. And I could feel everything everyone else felt as a consequence of my actions. Some of it felt good, and some of it felt awful. All of this translated into knowledge, and *I learned—Oh, how I learned!*

The information was flowing at an incredible speed that probably would have burned me up if it weren't for the extraordinary Energy holding me. The information came in, and then love neutralized my judgments against myself. In other words, information about every scene—my perceptions and feelings—and anyone else's perceptions and feelings that were in the scene came to me. No matter how I judged myself in each interaction, being held by God was the bigger interaction. God interjected love into everything, every feeling, every bit of information about absolutely everything that went on, so that everything was all right. There was no good and no bad. There was only me and my loved ones from this life trying to be or just trying to survive.

I realize now that without God holding me, I wouldn't have had the strength to experience what I did.

When it started, God and I were merging. We became one—so that I could see through God's eyes and feel through God's heart. Together, we witnessed how severely I had treated myself because that was the behavior shown and taught to me as a child. I realized that the only big mistake I had made in my life of thirty-two years was that I never learned to love myself. . . .

I also realized that I didn't end at my skin. We are all in this big churning mass of consciousness. We all seemed to be a part of this consciousness we call God. We're not just human. We are Spirit. We were Spirit before we came into this lifetime. We all seem to be struggling Spirits now, trying to get "being human" right. And when we leave here, we will be pure Spirit again.

God held me and let me into God's experience of all this. I felt God's memories of these scenes through God's eyes. I could sense God's divine intelligence, and it was astonishing. I know that God loves us and wants us to learn and to wake up to our True Self— to what is important. I realized that God wants us to know that we only experience real pain if we die without living first. And the way to live is to give love to ourselves and to others.

I experienced that we are here to learn to give and receive love. But only when we heal enough to be real can we understand and give and receive love the way love was meant to be.

When we are held by God in our life reviews and we merge into

One, we remember this feeling as being limitless. God is limitless. God's capacity to love is never-ending. God's love for us never changes, no matter how we are. God doesn't judge us. During our life review, we judge ourselves when we feel the pain we have created in other's lives. We also feel the love we have created in other's lives. (This may be a kind of "cosmic equalizer.")

I never saw an old man with a white beard sitting in judgment of me. I only felt limitless divine love. God interjected love into all the scenes of my life to show me God's reality. And the most amazing part of all is that God held nothing back. I understood all that God understood. God shared all of Godself with me—all the qualities of gentleness and openness and all the gifts . . . including the sudden experience of empowerment and peace. I never knew that much loving intelligence and freedom could exist. God held me in eternity.

I am back here, in time, but still with God. It is just a little harder for me to realize God's presence because my body and my mind get in the way. But that's all right. I still feel it as I continue to awaken to what is real—not the physical world that only teaches us to achieve and consume, but the real world where our spirits grow and learn about healing and love.

And now back in this lifetime, in this reality, what I learn about another person may not be what I had wanted that person to be. However, unconditional love remains firm. Real love begins only when one person comes to know another for who that person actually is as a human being. We get closer to the whole picture, the truth of who another is and *who we are.*

This reality now is interchangeable with my original life review. I am aware of God's presence, and I am aware that I have a choice of choosing pain or choosing love, choosing projection or expanding and becoming my potential. Each one of us is a unique reflection of God. *I sensed that for us not to develop to our potential is to deny God another facet of God's being.*[40]

TIME

Time and space are still different from the way they were before my near-death experience (see sidebar, "Time and Timelessness"). Daily, each relationship has the quality of my life review. I pray to create my life with God's energy of unconditional love. Each human relationship that I share with my Creator becomes the challenge of sustaining the higher levels or at least asking for the help to stay out of (or get out of) Level 1. And I am helped to hold some light so it can outshine the darkness.

I am learning to let go every moment and accept all of my experience—courage and fear, celebration and pain, expansiveness and limitation. Staying in touch and tender at the same time, this strength is coming from my core, or Child Within, in relationship to my Higher Self and Higher Power. Occasionally, for a moment, all three become One. Every one of us who struggles to learn unconditional love is giving birth to our Sacred Person. The faint inner voice that at one time we could barely hear, we now have more opportunities to embrace, bonding in unconditional love.

Time and Timelessness

At Levels 3 and 4 we realize there is no need to rush. We realize experientially that linear time is a construct of our intellect and has moved us to living on a horizontal line. Now we experience our reality and are connected in a *vertical* relationship with Spirit (God/Goddess/All-that-Is) and experience time in a vertical fashion that reveals a sense of the Eternal Now. We are like the giant oak tree—roots planted firmly in our physical bodies and our Spirits reaching like the huge branches stretching up to meet the heavens.

We still meet our appointments *on time* but our perception of time changes to give us a peaceful experience where we can focus on the task at hand and be fully present with it.

We have worked hard to heal our wounds, and in their place comes more than we expected. At this time in our own evolution, humility and gratitude give us a steady renewal that allows us to feel the abundance of the Universe. All our striving to become who God meant us to be—happens. As our physical being and our Spirit become one, our journey and destination become one—demonstrating the truth about duality and polarity. It was all an *illusion.* We are *One,* and separation collapses. We realize that peace and enjoyment are not a feeling but an attitude and a state of mind. We remember who we are and that we are already and always home. Even the belief in heaven *after* this lifetime recedes as we experience creating heaven here.[41]

And so it is at this Level 4 of human consciousness. We pass through this reality into the reality of God's bigger consciousness. We have moved from our limited experience and come face to face with the Universe. *At this level it is not simply that God chooses us, but that we also choose God.* We open to God every moment and with every breath. Then we choose to invite unconditional love, God's loving energy in action, into our lives. We live our own potential. And it hits us one day, possibly the day we notice that it is the same on both sides of reality: We are all inside God, and God is loving us through us.

I experience this as though I am holding one hand up to God in God's world and my other hand extended out to the people I love and the people I assist in their healing work. Other clinicians report similar observations during some sessions with their patients. Hospice workers and others who help people die report the same type of Level 4 experiences. One way to demonstrate this is while doing a hands-on healing (see sidebar, "Sharing the Energy of the Higher Levels" on page 139).

CREATION

We now realize that we are continuously creating our own reality instead of walking into one created for us by others or by default. We accept that we are a Sacred Person. Our True Self, joined to our Higher Self, is connected to our Higher Power so that instead of *Co-creating* as in Level 3, we are now at Level 4 *Creating* as our Sacred Person/God—with humility.

It is here that our joy lies. When we invite Spirit, Higher Self, into our conscious physical being, it brings with it what we have craved throughout our lives. We who at our core are Spirit need our root spiritual feelings—peace and joy. We naturally are Spirit—and these feelings of peace and joy are our natural spiritual feeling state when we open to and join with God to create our lives.

We are now *creating* our destinies. We remember our powers of manifestation and create our version of heaven on earth. No longer do we ask in prayer for what we want. We now proclaim gratitude for all we have, because instead of craving things, we witness the abundance already surrounding us. As we accomplish this, we automatically empower those around us, and everyone wins.

Our lives are a celebration because:

God has a dream

And the dream comes true—

Each time one of us

Awakens.

—*Barbara Whitfield*

CONCLUSION

In the Sermon on the Mount, Jesus says, "Blessed are the meek, for they shall inherit the earth." The Greek word for meek has been variously translated to include gentle, humble, considerate, patient, and courteous. Spiritual teacher and author Eckhart Tolle said, "The meek are the egoless. They are those that have awakened to their true nature as consciousness and recognize that essence in all 'others,' all life-forms. They live in the surrendered state and so feel their oneness with the whole and the Source. They embody the awakened consciousness that is changing all aspects of life on our planet, including nature, because life on earth is inseparable from the human consciousness that perceives and interacts with it. That is the sense in which the meek will inherit the earth. A new species is arising on the planet. It is arising now and you are it!"[42]

We take our conflicts and turn them into harmony. What seemed to be the curse becomes the gift. We make lemonade out of lemons. We transcend right and wrong, yin and yang, and unite our opposites. We heal the split and embrace something new, something born from balance. When all of us live life, sharing unconditional love, we may become the synergy of God. This is part of what the Mystery of God may include. It is not an easy task, but ultimately it is the one we may have been given. God's will is our highest human potential, shared.[43]

We summarized the characteristics of Level 4 and contrast them with the characteristics of Level 3 in Table 9.1. Please see Appendix E for expanded characteristics of the four levels.

Sharing the Energy of the Higher Levels

The type of healings I (BW) have written about in my previous books are an example of Level 3 and 4. A healing circle works like this: The person/patient receiving the energy is lying down and usually covered with a light blanket. Other members of the family, friends or health care team (who the receiver believes are "safe") gather around and sit with their hands gently and lightly touching the receiver. Before we begin, I say a prayer to unite and connect us in what we are asking to do. I say, "Dear God (or dear Holy Mother or whatever my patient feels comfortable with), please may we be *instruments* of your healing energy and your Oneness. Please help us to get our egos out of the way so you may come through."

This works with one person as an instrument or up to as many as six. The main principle is that the people who are doing the hands-on giving feel safe to the patient receiving the energy. We have had children as young as three in a healing circle and elders as old as ninety.

It doesn't matter if the people giving even believe in all this. All that matters is that we have the *intention* of wanting to help. Many times people receiving in a healing circle tell me afterward that their pain medication is working or that they don't need it now. Their skin coloring gets better, they are more relaxed and they feel loved. This can be done twice a day or more if the patient requests it.

The givers have often told me that the experience also calmed them. It not only helped their bodies to relax, it also helped their hearts to know they were giving "something" to the person in need. This is especially important to loved ones who before have been afraid to touch for fear of creating more pain. This gives them a safe way to express themselves that bypasses words.

We are not looking for a "cure." We are creating a sharing that brings comfort to the receiver—and usually spills over into the givers. Whether the patient is going to get better—or eventually die—isn't the point of these hands-on circles. Sharing universal love is the purpose.

We do this together for about twenty minutes. It feels like a meditation of clearing the mind and sitting in a peaceful way, placing our hands gently on the patient and sharing a current of energy that envelops all of us. We naturally come out of it in twenty minutes or so feeling more relaxed and at the same time energized because the energy we shared didn't come from us but came through us.

We close this healing circle with a prayer. "Dear God, dear Spirit, thank you for allowing us to be instruments of your healing energy. Thank you for allowing us to feel your Oneness. Amen."

Epilogue

"In the end—
only kindness matters!"

—*Jewel*

We are urgently in need of new ways to communicate in our relationships with ourselves, our significant others and our world. Millions are now living alone, unable to establish healthy relationships or unwilling to repeat the insane drama of past relationships. Still others compromise and continue to be together in dysfunctional relationships in which negativity prevails. As a nation, we are polarized, and this negativity filters down into our daily lives.

We began this book with quotes from some spiritual elders and indigenous peoples. As the Hopi Elders wrote:

It is time to speak your Truth.

Create your community.

Be good to each other.

And do not look outside yourself for the Leader.

This could be a good time! . . .

We are the ones we've been waiting for.

We believe that this is the time and that we are the ones. Each one of us can create a new community in our own personal world, and this new way can filter up into our work and our nation.

True communication includes communion. This then helps us realize that humility can move us up the levels of awareness and being until all there is is peace and love. If we can accept humility as a part of us, we can then accept that our relationships are here to make us *conscious*. Then our relationships will offer us a new kind of salvation, and we will be aligning ourselves with a greater awareness and consciousness that wants to be born into this world.

THE GIFTS OF HUMILITY

Living an authentic life with humility, we experience more gifts than can be listed here. The first one, however, is big. As shown in the map of the triangle levels on page vi and page 146, we now have a chance to become all of who we really are. As we practice working our way up the triangles, we experience ourselves in progressively expanded and more functional dimensions. This progression goes from false self (our major source of conflict) to True Self, and with spiritual practice, Higher Self, to joining in our natural birthright with our Higher Power.

We then learn that love is not selective, just as the light of the sun is not selective. It does not make one person special as Hollywood would have us believe. The love radiating from our True Self is grounded by humility. It becomes love for love's sake. At our core, we are Love.

HISTORY E.1: UNCONDITIONAL LOVE AND FORGIVENESS: MARSHALL AND BARBARA'S STORY

My brother and I (BW) were in a Level 1 triangle for a great deal of our lives. As children we seldom got along. As adults it was no better. We weren't conscious of the triangle until our mother died. But during our mourning period my sister-in-law told us, "Your mother always played one of you against the other. She was always making trouble between the two of you." That triangle was so embedded from my childhood on that I didn't even recognize it. However, looking back, it was always the three of us. My father never got involved. He was the typical enabler. Our mother, Marshall and I constantly changed positions being each other's victim, persecutor and rescuer. The roles often changed quickly.

Beginning around 1980, Marshall and I stopped talking to each other for more than nine years. We both believed we were right and the other wrong. We came from a clearly dysfunctional family. That was the real problem for both of us.

Around 1990, I was asked to do a talk at a hospital in Toledo, Ohio, about an hour and a half from where my brother lives. After nine years of silence, I picked up the phone and called him. He said he did want to see me and drove down after my talk and brought me back to his home. My three nieces were delighted to see me, and what took place was a great reunion that lasted five days (and a few nights where we sat up and talked until dawn).

We forgave each other without going into any of the past stories. Nine years had softened us—opened us to a new attitude of humility, something so different for those of us who grew up in dysfunctional homes. We gave each other unconditional love and we still do. He is who he is, and I am who I am. Forgiving was easy, but it took a lot of humility.

A few years ago, I was about to give a talk on forgiveness in Lake Arrowhead, California, for *A Course in Miracles* conference. It was Sunday morning. I was praying in my room as I always do before speaking. "Dear God, dear Holy Mother, please may I be an instrument of your wisdom and your healing energy. Please help me to get my ego out of the way so you can come through."

The phone rang. It was my brother. He said he had to call. He couldn't get me off his mind. I told him I was about to give a talk to three hundred people on forgiveness, and I was going to tell them our story. He answered with, "Now I know why I had to call you. Have a good talk, sweetheart. I love you!"

I started my talk with the conversation Marshall and I had just had. Then I told them our story of forgiveness and unconditional love. I received a standing ovation. Others stood and told of experiences they had forgiving their family members, and I heard more stories afterward throughout the whole conference. We all had miracles to share.

We each have miracles to share. Might you? You read this book. Perhaps you picked it up with some hope in your heart to make your life more peaceful and free of conflict. Writing this book made our lives better. We applied what we learned, and it worked. We offer you our best wishes for success with these new concepts. Our world needs each of us to bring humility and all its gifts here wherever we are.

MOVING TOWARD UNITY

In the simplest words and at whatever level of development, we are given a divine gift. At each moment, within each conflict that arises throughout our day, throughout our lives, we are given the power to choose. Do we choose to protect our point of view, our position and our ego's limited perceptions? Or through humility, do we choose not knowing, curiosity and tolerance? Do we choose to play the victim, to persecute or to rescue? Or through humility, do we choose to motivate, nurture and empower? Do we choose separation, or through humility, inclusion? Do we choose fear, or through humility, love? It's our humble choice.

The power of humility is the paradox that as we cultivate
and accept our "human-ness"—our humility—
we invite experiences of the Divine—peace,
love, joy, gratitude—into our lives and our relationships.

The power of humility is that it is the key to better relationships—
with self, others and God—and inner peace.

—*Charles and Barbara Whitfield*
—*Jyoti and Russell D. Park*

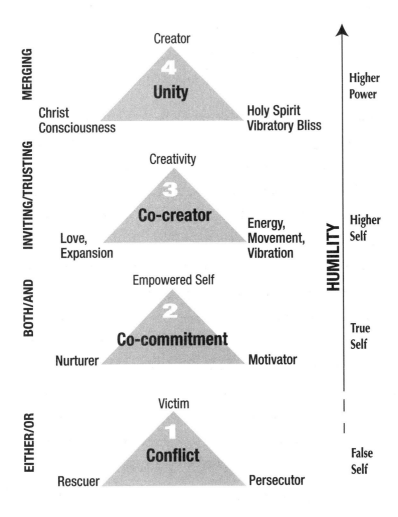

APPENDIX A:
QUOTES ON HUMILITY FROM
A COURSE IN MIRACLES

A Course in Miracles is a modern holy book that many people in recovery from various problems in living, including addictions and "mental illness," have found to be psychologically and spiritually nourishing. First published in 1976, it includes three volumes: a Text, a Workbook, and a Manual for Teachers. The entire Course addresses a major impediment to working through conflict and attaining peace by finding, accurately naming and letting go of our ego. The inflation and arrogance of ego is the opposite of humility.

The following are quotes from the Course that reference humility. These quotes are out of context from the flow in the Course, which is more circular than the conventional linear approach that we are used to reading and that we have incorporated in this book. We recommend that the reader study the Course itself to fully understand what these individual quotes say. We include them here as food for thought.

Humility is a lesson for the ego, not for the spirit. Spirit is beyond humility, because it recognizes its radiance and gladly sheds its light everywhere. The meek shall inherit the earth because their egos are humble, and this gives them truer perception. (T 4,1.12.2) (T=Text, 4=Chapter 4, 1=chapter section. 12=Paragraph, 2=Verse)

True empathy is of Him Who knows what it is [referring to the Holy Spirit]. You will learn His interpretation of it if you let Him use your capacity for strength, and not for weakness. He will not desert you, but be sure that you desert not Him. Humility is strength in this sense only; that to recognize and accept the fact that you do not know is to recognize and accept the fact that He *does* know. (T16, 1.1–4)

Humility will never ask that you remain content with littleness. But it does require that you be not content with less than greatness that comes not of you. Your difficulty with the holy instant arises from your fixed conviction that you are not worthy of it. And what is this but the determination to be as you would make yourself? God did not create His dwelling place unworthy of Him. (T18, 4.3.1–5)

Humility consists of accepting your role in salvation and in taking no other. It is not humility to insist you cannot be the light of the world if that is the function God assigned to you. It is only arrogance that would assert this function cannot be for you, and arrogance is always of the ego.

True humility requires that you accept today's idea because it is God's Voice which tells you it is true. This is a beginning step in accepting your real function on Earth. . . . "I am the light of the world. That is my only function. That is why I am here." (W61.2;2, 3 and 5). (W=Workbook)

To think that God made chaos, contradicts His Will, invented opposites to the truth and suffers death to triumph over life; all this is arrogance. Humility would see at once these things are not of Him.

Today we practice true humility, abandoning the false pretense by which the ego seeks to prove it arrogant. Only the ego can be arrogant. But truth is humble in acknowledging its mightiness, its changelessness and its eternal wholeness, all encompassing, God's perfect gift to his beloved Son. We lay aside the arrogance which says that we are sinners, guilty and afraid, ashamed of what we are; and lift our hearts in true humility instead to Him Who has created us immaculate, like to Himself in power and in love.

The power of decision is our own. And we accept of Him that which we are, and humbly recognize the Son of God. To recognize God's Son implies as well that all self-concepts have been laid aside, and recognized as false. Their arrogance has been perceived. And in humility the radiance of God's Son is gentleness, is perfect sinlessness, his Father's Love, his right to Heaven and release from hell, are joyously accepted as our own. (W152, 7–10)

All false humility we lay aside today, that we may listen to God's Voice reveal to us what He would have us do. . . . And if He deems us worthy, so we are. It is but arrogance that judges otherwise. (W186, 4)

In silence and in true humility I seek God's glory, to behold it in the Son whom He created as my Self. (W211, 2)

Let not the truth about ourselves today be hidden by a false humility. Let us instead be thankful for the gifts our Father gave us. (W239, 1)

And now sit down in true humility, and realize that all God would have you do you can do. Do not be arrogant and say you cannot learn His Own curriculum. (W14, 5:10–11)

For an introduction to the similarities between *A Course in Miracles* and the Twelve Steps, see also Appendix D on page 159.

APPENDIX B:
HUMILITY AND THE TWELVE STEPS:
THE SIXTH AND SEVENTH STEPS OF A.A.
AND OTHER TWELVE STEP FELLOWSHIPS

Step Six: We were entirely ready to have God remove all these defects of character.

Step Seven: Humbly asked Him to remove our shortcomings.[44]

Humility is crucial in working any Twelve Step program of recovery. Of the some 214 words that comprise the Twelve Steps, only one mentions humility directly: the first word in Step Seven. Even so, the importance of humility is implied and appears "between the lines" of all Twelve of these Steps. The opposite of humility—arrogance or ego inflation—are major blocks to recovery. This is why a humble attitude and authentic and heartfelt prayer assist us in working any program of recovery, including that of Twelve Step recovery fellowships.

We give the following as an example, which is taken with permission, from *The Little Red Book: An Interpretation of the Twelve Steps of the Alcoholics Anonymous Program:*[45]

It is only after we have completed Step Five, when humility has been experienced and self-respect has been restored as a result of our admitting to God and to another human being the exact nature of our wrongs, that we are in a suitable spiritual condition to sincerely carry out the provisions of Steps Six and Seven.

This action brings a heretofore unknown feeling of moral strength. For the first time we are facing our Real Selves [as illustrated in Figure 2.1 on page 16]—the selves whose withered roots have touched and are now drawing up an unfailing source of assurance, power and security.

We find in the consummation of these steps a *New Peace*, a release from *Tension* and Anxiety as we now are laying our misconceptions or defeats of character in God's hands. We are asking Him to rid them from our lives. We are exerting great mental cooperation with God. We feel an intense humility that cries out for recognition and Divine Help.

The *Spiritual Lift*, the nearness to our Creator that is experienced from humble invocation of His help and our willingness to be freed from old willful thoughts and habits are all essential to successful attainment of these steps.

The mental hygiene and spiritual housecleaning we have started in our inventories and continued in Step Five reaches its climax in Step Seven when we fully subject our wills to God and wish to surrender to Him all of our moral imperfections.

The several objectives of Steps Six and Seven are:

1. To gain an intimate contact with this Power Greater Than Ourselves.

2. To perfect ourselves in the practice of unselfish prayer.

3. To be aware of our defective character traits.

4. To desire their removal.

5. To surrender completely all defects of character.

6. To believe that God *can* remove them.

7. To ask Him to take them all away.

The results we expect from pursuit of these objectives are:

1. A reconciliation to God's way of doing business. We become "fed up" with our way and with further practice of our defective character traits.

2. A willingness to work out a plan for suppression of self-centeredness through gaining a conscious contact with God.

3. To experience dissatisfaction and remorse as a result of our alcoholic practices and to seek a spiritual inspiration that will bring us an inner sense of poise and security.

4. Increased faith, clean hearts and minds, ability to offer unselfish prayer.

5. A spiritual courage that is fearless in its outlook on life; a desire to make restitution to those our drinking has harmed.

6. A desire to quit bluffing and honestly give God a chance to remove from our lives all that stands in the way of our usefulness to Him and to others.

7. Elimination of our defective character traits, acquisition of peace of mind and sobriety.

The spiritual attitude and satisfactory frame of mind necessary to effective fulfilling of these steps has been progressively worked toward in the completion of the first five steps in our program. Knowledge of our illness, alcoholism, prompts us to turn to God for help. The alcoholic must pray. There is no standard form of prayer to use. Our remorse over past mistakes and a genuine desire to correct them will indicate how we shall pray.

We all come before God as sick people. We offer no alibis. We have no defense. We stand before Him subject to the weaknesses of alcoholism. We ask for an understanding of this illness and for His strength and help in arresting it. We wish to arrest it, but only for unselfish purposes. We ask forgiveness for the wrongs we have committed. We ask for protection from self-pity, from resentment, from all selfishness. We ask for wisdom and understanding to know His will. We ask for spiritual and physical strength to execute His will. Acknowledging our shortcomings, we sincerely pray to God that He will remove them.

Prayer is a three-way contact with God. By it we ask, receive and acknowledge. We thank Him now for our sobriety, for A.A. and its founders.

There is nothing outstanding about an alcoholic's prayer to God. It is just a simple sincere affair in which the alcoholic has nothing to lose but from which he gains. Sobriety—Sane Behavior—Peace of Mind—and Happiness for Himself and Family.

There is a latent power within each of us that develops through conscious contact with God. It replaces alcoholic fear and weakness with spiritual strength and understanding. Through It, the miracle of A.A. is possible.

Steps Six and Seven utilize this contact, which thousands of alcoholics have humbly used in removing their defects of character. In these two steps are found the forge in which we heat and form the separate links that go into the new personality chains we are building. *Without them our rehabilitation is impossible.*

Summarization—Restoration of our mental and spiritual health is in direct proportion to our recognized need for help and our willingness to work for recovery. Brain damage and reservations are the only limitations to our recovery.

Reservations are identified as those mental attitudes opposed to self-evaluation, cooperation, honesty, tolerance, forgiveness, faith, love and unselfish prayer. These "character defects" stand between us and contented sobriety. They perpetuate spiritual illness. Recovery from alcoholism is dependent upon their removal.

A divine type of surgery is suggested by Steps Six and Seven. Humble prayer becomes the spiritual scalpel with which God cuts out the damaged portions of our sick personalities. Complete surrender assures us a painless, successful operation.

Surrender of our "defects" to a "Higher Power" is not the spiritless act of a defeatist, but the intelligent act of an alcoholic who would replace his fear and weakness with spiritual courage, understanding, strength and contented sobriety. "Humbly ask Him to remove our shortcomings."

APPENDIX C:
QUOTES ON HUMILITY FROM
THE TWELVE STEPS AND TWELVE TRADITIONS
(excerpted from Alcoholics Anonymous, World Services, Inc.)

Commentary: Similar to *The Little Red Book,* the "12 and 12" also provides useful definitions and reflections on the power of humility, some of which we quote below.[46] From *page 30* (all of the following are direct quotes). . . . [AA members] showed us that humility and intellect could be compatible, provided you placed humility first.

Page 55. All of A.A.'s Twelve Steps ask us to go contrary to our natural desires... They all deflate our egos.

Page 70. . . . the attainment of greater humility is the foundation principle of each of A.A.'s Twelve Steps. . . . Many people haven't even a nodding acquaintance with humility as a way of life.

Page 71. . . . our crippling handicap had been our lack of humility. . . . material satisfactions were not the purpose of living.

Page 72. That basic ingredient of all humility, a desire to seek and do God's will, was missing. . . . It was only at the end of a long road, marked by successive defeats and humiliations, and the final crushing of our self-sufficiency, that we began to feel humility as something more than a condition of groveling despair.

Page 73. . . . to gain a vision of humility ...takes most of us a long, long time. A whole lifetime geared to self-centeredness can not be set in reverse all at once.

Page 74. We may still have no very high opinion of humility as a desirable personal virtue, but we do recognize it as a necessity to our survival. . . . our thinking about humility commences to have a wider meaning. . . . We enjoy moments in which there is something like real peace of mind. . . . Where humility had formerly stood for a forced feeding on humble pie, it now begins to mean the nourishing ingredient which can give us serenity.

Commentary: These sections from the 12 and 12 tell the recovering person more about how to strengthen their healing process. In clear words written by recovering alcoholics for others in pain these messages describe humility in further detail. It is remarkable how these early A.A.'s had such foresight and were able to discover and know so much about the power of humility.

Interspersed throughout these profound and practical writings are references to the need to identify our ego (false self) and to let go of our attachment to it. For example, we found still other references to this constructive use of humility, which we quote below.

Page 75. We heard story after story of how humility had brought strength out of weakness. . . . We began to fear pain less, and desire humility more than ever. . . . the most profound result of all was the change in our attitude toward God. We saw we needn't always be bludgeoned and beaten into humility. It could come quite as much from our voluntary reaching for it as it could from unremitting suffering. . . . we sought for humility as something we really wanted, rather than as something we must have. . . . we could commence to see the full implication of Step Seven: "Humbly asked Him to remove our shortcomings."

Page 76. We would like to be assured that the grace of God can do for us what we cannot do for ourselves. . . . The whole emphasis of Step Seven is on humility. . . . If that degree of humility could enable us to find the grace by which such a deadly obsession could be banished, then there must be hope of the same result respecting any other problem we could possibly have.

Page 187. . . . anonymity is real humility at work. It is an all-pervading spiritual quality which today keynotes A.A. life everywhere.

Authors' note: These quotes are but selected sentences that especially relate to these recovering people's understanding and use of the power of humility. We believe that this little book, *Twelve Steps* and *Twelve Traditions,* is outstanding. While we have quoted this allowable limited anount of text from the "12 and 12," we recommend that anyone interested consider reading it in its entirety.

APPENDIX D:
THE TWELVE STEPS AND *A COURSE IN MIRACLES*

Twelve Step fellowships such as Alcoholics Anonymous and over one hundred others, speak of what *A Course in Miracles* calls *special* (i.e., toxic or addicted) *relationships* in various ways. One is the trap that we get into called *resentments*. Almost by definition, when we have a resentment toward any person, place or thing, we are most likely to be enmeshed in such a special relationship. Not wanting to tolerate the emotional pain of the resentment, and not knowing what to do to heal it, we often search out our drug or behavior of choice to lessen the pain. But the Course says that there is a better way.

It says that whenever we may find ourselves involved in painful or conflicted relationships, we can remember that, as with any pain or conflict, we have a choice. We can choose God and then surrender into God's love and peace. The Course says that prayer is an effective tool to achieve this goal

There are numerous similarities between the Course and Twelve Step process and work. We show some of these similarities in Table D.1. Being spiritual seekers, many Twelve Steppers have begun to read and study the Course.

Table D.1: Similarity of Selected Terms from Twelve Step Work and *A Course in Miracles*

Alcoholics Anonymous	A Course in Miracles
2.* Sanity	Right mindedness; seeing with Christ's vision
3. Decision (made a . . .)	Decision maker; choice maker
4. Moral inventory process	ego undoing; forgiveness
5, 6 and 7. Our wrongs, character defects, shortcomings	ego attachment; wrong mind; mistakes
7. Humbly asked (humility)	Humility; openness; willingness
8 and 9. Making amends	Let go of ego/forgive
10. Continuing to take personal inventory	Vigilance for ego
11. Prayer and meditation	Prayer; miracles
Serenity	Inner peace

* Number of Step of A.A. and other self-help fellowships.

APPENDIX E:
FURTHER CHARACTERISTICS
OF THE FOUR LEVELS

Level 1 Thinking, Behaving and Being

Areas of Attention	Characteristics
Thought Process or Style	Negative thinking, either/or, all or none, black or white
Relationship with: Reality	Scarcity
Others	Compete
Higher Power	Fear, control, doubt, limiting, dependence
Feelings	Fear, confusion, guilt, shame
Desires	Addiction and attachment
View of the "Divine" (motivation)	Mother/father (programmed)
Other Names	Codependence, ego, separation, victim/martyr, controlling, shaming
Transformation of Suffering	Being "pushed by suffering"
Power Action (how you meet it)	Embrace the contrary, duality, opposites
Driving Energy	Desperation, survival drive (feminine); toxic frustration (masculine)
Spiritual practices	Conventional religion

Level 1 Thinking, Behaving and Being (cont'd)

Areas of Attention	Characteristics
Hindrances	Conventional religion, psychology, medicine, politics, business, media, mind control/ego, fear, doubt, shadow, intellectualization of life
Humility	Absent, arrogance and denial
Techniques for Raising	Conventional treatment, alcohol and drug treatment/Twelve Steps,
Levels of Awareness	Crisis or "hitting bottom"
Stage of Recovery	Conventional treatment approaches, Stage 0 = none
"Attitude" Toward Life	"No"
"Atman"	I (oneself)
"Action"	Sacrifice, martyr
"Attention"	Outward = Codependence, externally referenced
Stage of Hero's Journey	Separation

Level 2 Thinking, Behaving and Being

Areas of Attention	Characteristics
Thought Process or Style	Positive thinking = both/and, explore, accept
Relationship with:	
Reality	Abundance
Others	Cooperate
Higher Power	Exploration, possibility, expansion
Feelings	Satisfaction, brief happiness
Desires	Preferences
View of the "Divine" (motivation)	Guide, companion, choice
Other Names	Co-commitment, True Self
Transformation of Suffering	Pain—not suffering
Power Action (how you meet it)	Accept, balance
Driving Energy	Courage, leap of faith, longing for peace and unity
Spiritual Practices	Meditation, prayer, yoga, Twelve Step work, psychotherapy (humanistic, existential, transpersonal), body/breath work, indigenous practices
Hindrances	ego, shame, guilt, fear of abandonment or engulfment
Humility	Begins true expression

Level 2 Thinking, Behaving and Being (cont'd)

Areas of Attention	Characteristics
Techniques for Raising Levels of Awareness	Co-dependence education, alcohol and drug treatment, psychotherapy, Twelve Step continued
Stage of Recovery	Childhood trauma work
"Attitude" Toward Life	"Maybe"
"Atman"	Self *and* Us
"Action"	Sharing
"Attention"	Pain (not suffering)
Stage of Hero's Journey	Initiation

Level 3 Thinking, Behaving and Being

Areas of Attention	Characteristics
Thought Process or Style	Both/and, "owning" = self-responsibility
Relationship with:	
Reality	Beginning manifestation, create with thought
Others	Inspiration, creative
Higher Power	Direct experience, surrender, natural knowing
Feelings	Joy, peace, gratitude
Desires	Transcendence of pain/pleasure, actualize
View of the "Divine" (motivation)	Beloved, longing, surrender, commitment
Other Names	Co-Creative, Higher Self
Transformation of Suffering	Divine Intelligence, compassion, letting go
Power Action (How you meet it)	Accept, balance
Driving Energy	Grace, stillness
Spiritual Practices	Deep meditation, prayer, yoga, selfless service
Hindrances	Ego, fear of losing self and choices
Humility	Builds, expressed
Techniques for Raising Levels of Awareness	Meditation, prayer, breath work, art, dance

Areas of Attention	Characteristics
Stage of Recovery	Spiritual
"Attitude" Toward Life	"Yes"
"Atman"	We
"Action"	Karma yoga
"Attention"	Self, others and God
Stage of Hero's Journey	Return and individuation

Level 4 Thinking, Behaving and Being

Areas of Attention	Characteristics
Thought Process or Style	Non-duality thinking, Sacred Witness
Relationship with:	
Reality	Already exists, At-one-ment
Others	Attractor, creator
Higher Power	Absorption, innocence
Feelings	Unconditional love, compassion, humility, completion
Desires	None
View of the "Divine" (motivation)	Oneness, "I Am," living God's will
Other Names	Higher Power, home, unity consciousness
Transformation of Suffering	Unconditional love, pulled by your vision
Power Action (how you meet it)	Vehicle of the Mystery
Driving Energy	Love in action, service, compassion
Spiritual Practices	Life
Hindrances	Pressure of the collective unconsciousness
Humility	Is fully expressed
Techniques for Raising Levels of Awareness	Grace and divine intervention, Mystery School models, go to the abbey, student lives with teacher

Level 4 Thinking, Behaving and Being (cont'd)

Areas of Attention	Characteristics
"Attitude" toward life	"Yes"
"Atman"	All
"Action"	Divine will, selfless service
"Attention"	Inward, divine absorption, God centered
Stage of Hero's Journey	The hero returns

NOTES

1. Kundalini Research Network: International Symposium Proceedings, Oct. 15-18, Atlanta, Georgia; Karen Barsell, LCSW, Russell Park, PhD, Jyoti (Prevatt) *From Co-dependency to the Holy Trinity.*

2. Fogarty T: "On Emptiness and Closeness, Part 1: The Distancer and the Pursuer." *Compendium One. Center for Family Learning.* (1978–83). (Several papers, including the following); Fusion; Triangles; Evolution of a Systems Thinker. New Rochelle, NY.

3. Ring K: *Lessons from the Light: What We Can Learn from the Near-Death Experience* (New York: Insight Books, 1998).

4. Deikman A J: *The Observing Self* (Boston: Beacon Press, 1982).

5. Juigla K: *Mellennial Twins: An Esssay into Time and Place Revision,* Vol 22, number 3, pp. 29–43.

6. The Hopi Indians have an oral tradition. We know this was said at a meeting of the Elders at Oraibi, Arizona, in 2000.

7. Random House Dictionary 1980, Oxford 1971.

8. Translation by Richard B. Clarke of the *Hsin Hsin Ming.* The Coach House Press Toronto, Canada 1973.

9. Foundation for Inner Peace, *A Course in Miracles* (New York: Viking, 1996).

10. Ibid., W339, 4:3–4.

11. Ibid., T41, 7:1.

12. Ibid., T41, 7:4.

13. Tolle E: *The Power of Now: A Guide to Spiritual Enlightenment* (Novato, CA: New World Library, 1999).

14. Foundation for Inner Peace, *A Course in Miracles* (New York: Viking, 1996).

15. Ibid., and Tolle E., *The Power of Now: A Guide to Spiritual Enlightenment* (Novato, CA: New World Library, 1999).

16. Tolle E: *The Power of Now: A Guide to Spiritual Enlightenment* (Novato, CA: New World Library, 1999).

17. Smith H: *The Religions of Man* (New York: Harper & Row, 1958).

18. Yoshinori T: *Buddhist Spirituality* Crossroads (New York:): p. 4, 59, 75, 305

19. Whenary R: *The Texture of Being* (UK: Lotus Harmony Publishing Totnes, 2000) see *www.lotusharmony.com*

20. Ram Dass, Levine S: *Grist for the Mill* (Santa Cruz, CA: Unity Press, 1996).

21. Whitfield CL, *Healing the Child Within: Discovery and Recovery for Adult Children of Dysfunctional Families* (Deerfield Beach, FL: Health Communications, Inc., 1987); and *Boundaries and Relationships: Knowing, Protecting and Enjoying the Self* (Deerfield Beach, FL: Health Communications, Inc., 1993).

22. As described in Chapters 13 and 14, Whitfield C: *Boundaries and Relationships: Knowing, Protecting and Enjoying the Self* (Deerfield Beach, FL: Health Communications, Inc., 1993).

23. For further discussion on fusion, see C. Whitfield, *Boundaries and Relationships: Knowing, Protecting and Enjoying the Self* (Deerfield Beach, FL: Health Communications, Inc., 1993).

24. Whitfield CL, J Silberg and P Fink, eds., *Misinformation Concerning Child Sexual Abuse and Adult Survivors* (New York: Haworth Press, 2002).

25. Whitfield B: *Spiritual Awakenings: Insights of the Near-Death Experience and Other Doorways to Our Soul* (Deerfield Beach, FL: Health Communications, Inc., 1995).

26. As Tom Forgarty describes in CL Whitfield: *Boundaries and Relationships: Knowing, Protecting and Enjoying the Self.* (Deerfield Beach, FL: Health Communications, Inc., 1993) p: 180).

27. Whitfield CL: *Memory and Abuse: Remembering and Healing the Effects of Trauma* (Deerfield Beach, FL: Health Communications, Inc., 1995).

28. Whitfield CL: *A Gift to Myself: A Personal Workbook and Guide to Healing the Child Within* (Deerfield Beach, FL: Health Communications, Inc., 1990).

29. Kerr ME, Bowen M: *Family Evaluation: An Approach Based on Bowen Theory* (New York: WW Norton, 1988).

30. Karpman SB: "Fairy tales and Script Drama Analysis," *Transactional Analysis Bulletin* 7.26: 39–40, (April 7, 1968).

31. Ibid.

32. From Whitfield CL: *Boundaries and Relationships: Knowing, Protecting and Enjoying the Self,* (Deerfield Beach, FL: Health Communications, Inc., 1993) p: 180.

33. While Bowen and his colleagues have used the word "differentiation" as a major concept in their theory and their work, Bowen himself never fully explained the term. He did say that poorly differentiated people have a high percentage of life problems, such as physical and emotional illness, social maladaption and failures. Well-differentiated people's thinking and feeling functions are more differentiated and autonomous; they have fewer life problems, are more successful in life, have more energy to devote to their own life courses, and their relationships are more free and intimate. Basic level or differentiation describes, among other things, functioning that is not dependent on the emotionally driven process of being in a

relationship. Although he had initially hoped that the general population would be distributed evenly over a scale of poorly to well differentiated people, he concluded that about 90 percent of them were in the lower end and perhaps 10 percent of them were well-differentiated. My (CW) sense is that Bowen's idea of "well differentiated" is nearly the same as "self-actualized" and close to what we would call being in an advanced level of Stage Two recovery.

34. For some healing exercises around secrets, see Chapter 13, Whitfield CL: *A Gift to Myself: A Personal Workbook and Guide to Healing the Child Within* (Deerfield Beach, FL: Health Communications, Inc., 1990).

35. Geffner R: editorial in *Family Violence & Sexual Assault Bulletin* 20.4 (Winter 2004).

36. Hendricks G, Hendricks K: *Conscious Loving: The Journey to Co-Commitment.*

37. For more on learning to tolerate emotional pain, see Whitfield CL: *A Gift to Myself: A Personal Workbook and Guide to Healing the Child Within* (Deerfield Beach, FL: Health Communications, Inc., 1990); and Whitfield CL: *My Recovery: A Personal Plan for Healing* (Deerfield Beach, FL: Health Communications, Inc., 2003).

38. We are here referring more to a level of consciousness than the historical figure.

39. I (BW) am referring here to my near-death experience. I had a life review in which I was able to see and experience my life over again. In that review I was able to experience everything that others felt, so that in a strange but awesome way, I was not only me—I was them, too. And God was also showing me all this through God's eyes.

40. Whitfield BH: *The Natural Soul* (in process) also see Dana Iujoki's "A Return to Natural Time," *Planetlightworker.com* Dec 04.

41. Whitfield BH: Ibid.

42. Tolle E: *The Power of Now: A Guide to Spiritual Enlightenment* (Novato, CA: New World Library, 1999).

43. Whitfield BH: *Spiritual Awakenings: Insights of the Near-Death Experience and Other Doorways to Our Soul* (Deerfield Beach, FL: Health Communications, Inc., 1995).

44. Note paragraphs 2 and 3, page 88, in *Alcoholics Anonymous.* (New York, NY; aa World Services Inc).

45. Alcoholics Anonymous: *The Little Red Book: An Interpretation of the Twelve Steps of the Alcoholics Anonymous Program* (Center City, MN: Hazelden, 195:87–92).

46. Alcoholics Anonymous, *Twelve Steps and Twelve Traditions* (New York: Alcoholics Anonymous World Services, Inc.,1952–1981).

REFERENCES

Alcoholics Anonymous. *Twelve Steps and Twelve Traditions.* New York: Alcoholics Anonymous World Services, Inc.,1952–1981.

Avruj A: *Fear of Light.* Unpublished manuscript.

Deikman AJ: *The Observing Self.* Boston: Beacon Press, 1982.

Fogarty T F: "On Emptiness and Closeness, Part 1: The Distancer and the Pursuer." Compendium One. Center for Family Learning (1978–83). (Several papers, including the following); Fusion; Triangles; Evolution of a Systems Thinker. New Rochelle, NY.

Foundation for Inner Peace. *A Course in Miracles.* New York: Viking, 1996.

Geffner R: *Family Violence & Sexual Assault Bulletin* 20.4 (Winter 2004).

Hendricks G, Hendricks K: *Conscious Loving: The Journey to Co-Commitment.* New York: Bantam, 1992.

Hoffman J: "After Enlightenment, What Next?" *Planetlightworker.com.* August 2004. (also see www.urielheals.com)

Iujoki D: "A Return to Natural Time." *Planetlightworker.com.* 2004. (Also see: *www.danamrkich.com.*)

Jyoti: *An Angel Called My Name.* Prague: DharmaGaia, 1998.

Lansdowne ZF: *The Chakras & Esoteric Healing.* York Beach, Maine: Samuel Weiser, 1986.

Motoyama H: *Theories of the Chakras: Bridge to Higher Consciousness.* Wheaton, IL: Quest Books, 1981.

Naranjo C: *Character and Neurosis: An Integrative View.* Gateway Books and Tapes, 1994.

Planetlightworker.com. An Internet magazine with cutting edge spiritual and personal growth articles. Highly recommended.

Ram Dass, S Levine: *Grist for the Mill.* Santa Cruz, CA: Unity Press, 1996.

Renee L: *Energeticsynthesis.com,* 2006

Ring K: *Lessons from the Light: What We Can Learn from the Near-Death Experience.* New York: Insight Books, 1998.

Schwartz GER. et al. "Loving Openness as a Meta-World Hypothesis: Expanding Our Vision of Mind and Medicine." *Advances in Mind-Body Medicine* (John E. Fetzer Institute) 15 (1999): S-19.

Tolle E: *The Power of Now: A Guide to Spiritual Enlightenment.* Novato, CA: New World Library, 1999.

Tolle E: *A New Earth*. New York: Dutton, 2005.

Trout S: *The Awakened Healer,* Alexandria, VA: Three Roses Press, 2005.

Whenary R: "Diving Into the Bliss." *Planetlightworker.com.*

———. *The Texture of Being.* UK: Lotus Harmony Publishing, 2005. (*www.lotus publishing.com*)

Whitfield B: *Final Passage: Sharing the Journey as This Life Ends.* Deerfield Beach, FL: Health Communications, Inc., 1998.

———. *Spiritual Awakenings: Insights of the Near-Death Experience and Other Doorways to Our Soul.* Deerfield Beach, FL: Health Communications, Inc., 1995.

Whitfield B: *The Natural Soul* (in process).

Whitfield B, and L. Bascom: *Full Circle: The Near-Death Experience and Beyond.* New York: Simon and Schuster Pocket Books, 1990.

Whitfield CL: *Alcoholism, Attachments and Spirituality: A Transpersonal Approach.* Rutherford, NJ: private printing, 1985.

———. *Boundaries and Relationships: Knowing, Protecting and Enjoying the Self.* Deerfield Beach, FL: Health Communications, Inc., 1993. (Also translated and published in French and Spanish editions.)

———. *Co-dependence: Healing the Human Condition.* Deerfield Beach, FL: Health Communications, Inc., 1991.

———. *A Gift to Myself: A Personal Workbook and Guide to Healing the Child Within.* Deerfield Beach, FL: Health Communications, Inc., 1990. (Also translated and published in a French edition.)

———. *Healing the Child Within: Discovery and Recovery for Adult Children of Dysfunctional Families.* Deerfield Beach, FL: Health Communications, Inc., 1987. (Also translated and published in French, German, Spanish, Italian, Greek, Portuguese, Farsi, Japanese, Croatian and Korean translation editions.)

———. *Memory and Abuse: Remembering and Healing the Effects of Trauma.* Deerfield Beach, FL: Health Communications, Inc., 1995

———. *My Recovery: A Personal Plan for Healing.* Deerfield Beach, FL: Health Communications, Inc., 2003

———. *The Truth About Depression: Choices for Healing.* Deerfield Beach, FL: Health Communications, Inc., 2003 (also translated and published in Portuguese)

———. *The Truth About Mental Illness: Choices for Healing.* Deerfield Beach, FL: Health Communications, Inc., 2004

Whitfield CL, Silberg J Fink, P. (eds). *Misinformation Concerning Child Sexual Abuse and Adult Survivors.* New York: Haworth Press, 2002

Wolinski K. *Letting Go with All Your Might.* Denver, CO: ReDecisions Institute, 1995

ABOUT THE AUTHORS

Charles L. Whitfield, M.D., is a pioneer in addictions and in trauma recovery, including the way we remember childhood and other trauma and abuse. A physician and frontline therapist who assists trauma survivors in their healing, he is the author of over sixty published articles and ten bestselling books on trauma psychology and recovery. Four of these books have been translated and published in ten foreign languages. Since 1995 he has been voted by his peers as being one of the best doctors in America. For over twenty-three years he has taught at Rutgers University's Institute on Alcohol and Drug Studies. He is a consultant and research collaborator at the Centers for Disease Control and Prevention since 1998. He has a private practice in Atlanta, Georgia, with his wife, Barbara, where they provide individual and group therapy for trauma survivors and people with addictions and other problems in living. For more information go to *www.cbwhit.com* and *www.barbarawhitfield.com*.

Barbara H. Whitfield, R.T., C.M.T., is the author of many published articles and five books. She is a thanatologist (thanatology is the study of death and dying), workshop presenter, near-death experiencer and respiratory and massage therapist. She was on the faculty of Rutgers University's Summer School for Alcohol and Drug Studies for twelve years. Barbara was research assistant to psychiatry professor Bruce Greyson at the University of Connecticut Medical School, studying the psychological, physical and energetic aftereffects of the near-death experience. She is past president and a member of the board of the Kundalini Research Network and has sat on the executive board of the International Association for Near-Death Studies. She is a consulting editor and contributor for the *Journal of Near-Death Studies.* Barbara has been a guest on major television talk shows including *Larry King Live, The Today Show, Man Alive, Donahue, Unsolved Mysteries, Good Morning America, Oprah,* and *CNN Medical News.* Her story and her research have appeared in documentaries in the United States, Canada, Japan, France, Belgium and Italy and in magazines such as *Redbook, McCalls, Woman's World, McClean's, Common Boundary, Psychology Today* and others. For more information go to *www.cbwhit.com.*

Russell D. Park, Ph.D., is a clinical psychologist specializing in transpersonal psychology and neurotherapy. Russell is a contract faculty member for the Institute of Transpersonal Psychology and the Union Institute. As the former research coordinator for the Spiritual Emergence Network founded by Stan and Christina Grof, Russell has taught professionals in Europe, South America, and the United States in the diagnosis, treatment and transformative potential of spiritual emergence phenomena. In addition, he has a background in clinical laboratory medicine, alternative healing approaches, biotechnology research, and computer science applications and practices. Other interests include personal empowerment, the interface between psychology and spirituality, drug addictions, and the use of visual and auditory media for psychological change. Russell, together with his wife, Jyoti, teaches seminars and workshops on transformational process to an international community of professionals.

Jyoti (Jeneane Prevatt, Ph.D.) is internationally known as a spiritual and psychological consultant working with spiritual emergence as it manifests through the individual and community. She has explored multicultural approaches that raise consciousness in the body, resulting in a healing of body, mind and spirit. Her spiritual and psychological insights provide a balanced approach to integrating one's life. Her extensive study of indigenous healing and spiritual practices combined with her training in Jungian and psychological approaches to mental health have inspired a variety of projects. Her consistent focus is to actively affirm our role as guardians of this planet, consciously creating communities, through business and social reform, that bring heart and divine intention to the forefront. She resides in Sonora, California, and travels, lecturing, across the United States, Europe and South America. See also *www.mothersgrace.com*.

Index

Also from
Charles L. Whitfield

Dr. Whitfield in *Healing the Child Within* describes the journey of healing our fears, confusion and unhappiness.

Code #440 • $14.95

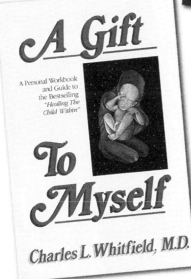

This is a gentle and effective workbook and guide to *Healing the Child Within*.

Code #2335 • $12.95

Books from
Barbara Harris Whitfield

FINAL PASSAGE

Whether you fear death because it symbolizes the unknown, marvel at its awesome mystery, or grieve for a loved one it has claimed, this book will answer your questions about what happens when we die.

Sharing the Journey as This Life Ends

Barbara Harris Whitfield

Code #5408 • $10.95

Foreword by Charles L. Whitfield, M.D.

SPIRITUAL AWAKENINGS

INSIGHTS OF THE NEAR-DEATH EXPERIENCE AND OTHER DOORWAYS TO OUR SOUL

Barbara Harris Whitfield

Code #3383 • $8.95

Barbara Harris Whitfield shares her own story and the stories of others who have encountered near-death experiences and explores why they have such a powerful effect on people.